1690

William and the Boyne

*Other books by Ian Adamson
available from Pretani Press*

Bangor, Light of the World
The Cruthin
The Identity of Ulster
The Ulster People

1690

William and the Boyne

Ian Adamson

First published by **Pretani Press**, 1995
17 MAIN STREET, CONLIG
NEWTOWNARDS BT23 3PT

A Nosmada Book

Typeset by Island Publications, Newtownabbey
Printed in Northern Ireland by The Universities Press (Belfast) Ltd

ISBN   0 948868 20 1

This book is dedicated to the memory of my friend and colleague
René Fréchet, 1910–1992

René Fréchet was, for many years, the voice of Ireland in Paris. Professor of English at the Sorbonne and founder, in 1979, of the University's Institute of Irish Studies, he served as guide and counsellor to the growing number of students who chose an Irish theme for their research. His *History of Ireland* (University Press, Paris, 1970) is merely one facet amongst many others of his vast knowledge of things Irish: published articles (particularly in *Réforme*), lectures and translations.

He spared no effort to encourage visits to Paris by Irish poets, novelists and essayists in order to show the most varied examples of the living reality. Thanks to his encouragements and scrupulous attendance at all the conference centres around Ireland, his name, in France and abroad, invariably evoked the Emerald Isle.

In addition to his love of Irish literature – his translation of Yeats' poetry (Aubier, 1989) is a model of precision and sensitivity – he kept in close touch with events in Northern Ireland. His interest was shaped by an acute knowledge of facts and an unfailing affection for the region. As a young lecturer, he spent two years at Queen's University, Belfast: the experience he acquired, and the lasting friendships he established, gave him an indisputable authority to comment on that unhappy state of affairs.

For Ulster Protestants he was certainly the most respected spokesman in France: his convictions and courageous declarations counterbalanced the somewhat superficial presentations of the French national press with regard to this community. At the time of his sudden death he was preparing to translate the recent work of Ian Adamson, *The Ulster People*. The notes he left are a testimony to his mastery of the subject.

Distinguished by the truly Protestant virtues of diligence, sincerity and integrity, he was a reserved man, reminiscent of one of the writers he most admired, "that slow and meditative man", according to Yeats: John Synge.

The death of René Fréchet deprives France of a remarkable teacher, a perceptive critic, a brilliant translator and most of all, of an incomparable expert on Modern Ireland, whilst his adoptive country has lost one of its most faithful, passionate and lucid friends.

Above all, his many friends and admirers will miss a man who, throughout his rich and productive life, was the personification of sincerity and loyalty.

Mark Mortimer
Department of English
Université de Paris III
Sorbonne Nouvelle.

The author would like to thank his family, friends and colleagues for their support and encouragement over the years. Their opinions, however, are not necessarily those held by the author, who is solely responsible for the views expressed in this book.

Contents

Introduction

— A Broader Perspective—

In her book *The Crack–A Belfast Year* Sally Belfrage recounted a conversation she had with a young Protestant boy, whose family had taken her to see the annual 'Twelfth of July' Orange parade through Belfast:

> The seven-year-old... and I had tea. He decided to try his mixed with orange drink. It was delicious, he said.
> "What do you think the parade was for?" I asked him.
> "Nuthin'," he said, stirring his brew.
> "What about King William?"
> "He's dead."
> "Do you know anything about him?"
> "He was popular," said James.
> "Who with?"
> "With the Queen."
> "What was her name?"
> "I dunno. Maybe Queen William of Orange."
> "Oh. Do you know anything else about him?"
> "He owned all the orange things. Every single thing. All them bands belonged to him. He owned them clothes the bands was wearing."
> "But some of the suits were different colours. Your dad's is purple."
> "He doesn't own me *da's*." He looked at me as if I were a half-wit. "He only owns the bands with *orange* suits. Everything in this world what is orange he owns. He could tell me to give him that bottle," he said, pointing at the source of half the concoction he was drinking. "And he could tell you to give him that pen. And that," he said, "is all I know about him." [1]

Now we may smile amusedly at such a conversation, ascribing the boy's naivety to childhood innocence, yet it has to be admitted that in Ireland quite a few adults retain an equally circumscribed understanding of King William and 'the Boyne'. This pertains even among some of King William's present-day followers: a prominent journalist once remarked that when one of his colleagues decided to question Orangemen about the history of their movement, he "received the most outlandish answers". [2]

Furthermore, like that child, who saw King William as not just a vague character from history, but someone who could have a direct impact upon his own life – "He could tell me to give him that bottle" – for many adults, and the communities to whom they give allegiance, King William still 'lives', retaining a present-day vitality which belies the 300 years which have passed since his moment in history. This living relevance is not confined to King William's modern supporters – the Protestants of Ulster – but includes the present-day descendants of his former adversaries – the Catholics of Ireland, particularly those in Ulster. For in all games of 'heroes and villains' one man's 'hero' can only retain his potency when he is simultaneously demonised as another's 'villain'.

The problem for Ireland has always been that in this historical 'game' the combatants have continued to play their parts with serious intent, and with deadly repercussions. 'Remember William and the Boyne!' became a shibboleth which inspired many a Loyalist throughout Ulster's tragic strife, just as a desire – whether spoken or unspoken – to undo the consequences of William's victory became a motivating factor for many Nationalists.

It is time, then – indeed, some would say that time is long overdue – to take a closer look at William and the Boyne, to try and disentangle myth from reality, to see that period of our history in its broadest perspective, to clarify just what was at stake for the participants as the events unfolded, and explore just *who* those participants in Ireland really were.

This is not an attempt to 'rewrite' the story of William and the Boyne, merely an effort to paint it on a larger canvas, so that a better informed and more realistic appraisal can be made of its significance.

Such a broadening of perspective may not be to everyone's liking – both supporters and detractors of King William alike often share a vested interest in retaining the simplistic version of his story which reinforces their present-day attitudes. Those Catholics for whom William personifies 'English oppression' might not care to learn that he endeavoured to be fairer to their forebears than the English ruling establishment would allow him, as the incident of the 'missing clause' reveals. Those Protestants who see William as the embodiment

*Painting formerly believed to depict King William's crusade
being blessed by Pope Innocent XI*

of their undying loyalty to England might be surprised to know that he was once so irritated with the English parliament he considered abdicating and returning to his native Holland. Those Catholics who imagine that William was motivated by anti-Catholicism might be disconcerted to learn that he was actually in alliance with the Pope, who helped finance his struggle against James. Those Protestants who imagine that it was the Battle of the Boyne which secured 'religious liberty' for their forefathers might be surprised to learn that in the period following the 'Glorious Revolution' the intense harassment suffered by Irish Presbyterianism at the hands of the English High Church was a major factor compelling thousands upon thousands of Ulster Protestants to emigrate to the new land of America, where their estrangement from Britain moulded them into the staunchest exponents of rebellion against the Crown and the most militant of adversaries in the American War of Independence. Those ethnic purists – whether Protestant or Catholic – who like to imagine the combatants at the Boyne as representing two quite distinct peoples – 'Planter' and 'Gael' – might feel uncomfortable on learning that the ancient kinship between the religious antagonists was much closer than most people could have imagined.

What purpose should a book such as this set out to accomplish? Well, for a start, there does not need to be any specific purpose – to provide a broader perspective on the Boyne period is sufficient justification in itself. However, as all my previous work has been aimed at creating an awareness among the Ulster people of the commonality of their historical and cultural heritage, I will not deny that I harbour the hope that such a broadening of perspective will help dilute some of the power of '1690 and the Boyne' to inflame sectarian passions – from whatever quarter – and allow the present (and future) citizens of Ulster and Ireland to integrate that period of their history less emotively – and less divisively – into the rich tapestry which makes up their unique historical inheritance. For we are indeed a very fortunate people – the marvellous diversity of both Irish and British culture has been accorded to us. We should all be proud of what we are.

1

— The Irish Antagonists —

One unfortunate tendency in many books about the Boyne is that they invariably end too abruptly – usually bringing the story to a close with the departure from Ireland of Sarsfield's defeated but courageous 'Wild Geese' after the fall of Limerick – and scant mention is made of the political, religious and social after-effects in Ireland and abroad. More fundamentally, perhaps, these books invariably *begin too late*. Just like King William himself, the reader is thrust into an Ireland apparently peopled by citizens ripe for religious conflict, with no attempt made by the author, other than in a superficial manner, to explain anything to us about their ethnic background, except to suggest that they were somehow 'alien' to each other. We are left feeling, as popular imagery would still have it today, that William and James were rather fortunate, in the midst of a somewhat complex European conflict, to have found a battleground where two apparently distinct and separate tribes were only too eager to rally to the standards of the opposing sides.

However, given that the story of the Boyne has already proven it can reach far beyond the confines of its historical period, and accepting that it is important to lay to rest many of the myths associated with it if we are ever to exorcise its divisive character, then I think it is perfectly acceptable to start right at the beginning.

The Battle of the Boyne is believed, in its crudest popular associations, to represent the ultimate trial of strength between 'Planter' and 'Gael' – with these Planters being 'aliens' who made their first appearance on Irish soil when they were imported from Scotland during the 17th century Plantation, and with the Gaels having been in Ireland from time immemorial. However, when we go back to the 'beginning' – and here we mean the Stone Age – we not only see the peoples of Ireland and Scotland already evidencing close contact with each other, but the Gaels have still to make an appearance.

The first settlers came to Ireland around 6,500 BC, in the period known as the Mesolithic Age, archaeological evidence suggesting that they probably came from the Galloway region of Scotland or Cumbria in northern England to the east coast of Ulster.[3] In the following Neolithic period the inhabitants have left us widespread evidence of their presence, in the form of intriguing stone burial monuments, such as *dolmens* and *court cairns*. Some of Europe's largest and most impressive Stone Age monuments are those erected by the Neolithic Irish in the Boyne valley, the best known being the great passage tomb at Newgrange. The *court cairns*, which are distributed mainly around the northern half of Ireland, are also found in south-west Scotland, leading Séan O Ríordáin to comment: "The tombs and the finds from them form a continuous province joined rather than divided by the narrow waters of the North Channel."[4]

Such a link is hardly surprising. With Ireland and Scotland separated, at their closest points, by only thirteen miles, and considering that much of the land was covered with dense forest, the North Channel of the Irish Sea would have acted not as a barrier but rather as an effective means of communication. Indeed, commenting on the archaelogical evidence for contact across the Irish Sea, John Waddell suggested:

> We may be seeing just the archaeologically visible elements of a much more complex pattern of social interaction across and around the Irish Sea. Perhaps we have greatly underestimated the extent to which this body of water linked the two islands in prehistoric times.[5]

The entrance stone to the Newgrange tomb

14

The earliest known reference to the British Isles, made between 330 and 300 BC by the Greek geographer and voyager Pytheas in his *Concerning the Ocean*, describes them as the *Isles of the Pretani*, the 'Pretani' thus becoming the most ancient inhabitants of Britain and Ireland to whom a definite name can be given. In Ireland these ancient British Pretani (or Britanni) were later to become known as *Cruthin*, while in Scotland they became known as *Picts*. In the writings of the medieval Irish it is clear a definite kinship was believed to have existed between these ancient peoples. We are not in a position to ascertain the full extent of their relationship, but the proximity of north-east Ulster to south-west Scotland, coupled with the archaeological evidence of ongoing contact, would certainly lend weight to the strong possibility that it was very close. Indeed, as Liam de Paor has commented:

> The gene pool of the Irish... is probably very closely related to the gene pools of highland Britain... Within that fringe area, relationships, both cultural and genetic, almost certainly go back to a much more distant time than that uncertain period when Celtic languages and customs came to dominate Great Britain and Ireland. Therefore, so far as the physical make-up of the Irish goes... they share these origins with their fellows in the neighbouring parts – the north and west – of the next-door island of Great Britain. [6]

So here we have our first anomaly: the peoples of Ireland and Scotland, who, in popular imagery, are deemed to have had only minimal contact with each other prior to the 17th century Plantation and are assumed to be of quite different ethnic stock, in reality show evidence of extensive contact as far back as the Stone Age, and scholars now acknowledge that in all probability the two peoples share a close cultural and genetic inheritance.

Scholars also accept that both peoples owe their predominant ancestry to their pre-Celtic past, an ancestry consolidated during the Neolithic period. It is now believed that any intrusions into Ireland which occurred subsequent to this period involved relatively small numbers of people. This applies even when we consider the Celts. A seminar held by the Irish Association of Professional Archaeologists in 1984 acknowledged that any Celtic intrusions into Ireland were more than probably carried out by numbers "far inferior to the native population(s)". [7] As archaeologist Peter Woodman has pointed out:

15

The gene pool of the Irish was probably set by the end of the Stone Age when there were very substantial numbers of people present and the landscape had already been frequently altered. The Irish are essentially Pre-Indo-European, they are not physically Celtic. No invasion since could have been sufficiently large to alter this fact completely. [8]

Liam de Paor also asked:

But was there a displacement of population, with tall, blond, blue-eyed Celts coming to take over from the small dark people (if such they were) of Mesolithic and Neolithic origin? Not at all. The Celts were, at best, the Ascendancy of their day, a minority powerful enough to impose their language. [6]

We cannot be certain as to when the first groups of Celtic people arrived in Ireland, but it is now clear that, contrary to a once popular belief, they were not present in Ireland from time immemorial, and are – in historical terms – of much more recent origin. At present there is no evidence which can place Celtic settlement in Ireland, as characterised by intrusive burial customs, before the 1st century AD. However, despite their small numbers, the Celts, particularly those known to us as the Gaels, soon acquired a dominant position in Irish political life, perhaps because of their martial skills, perhaps because of the dynastic manner in which they divided out their conquests.

Once Gaelic power had begun to consolidate itself, their most important dynasty, the Uí Néill, embarked upon the conquest of the north of the island, the territory associated with the ancient province of Ulster. The progress of this conquest, however, was resisted by the pre-Celtic Cruthin population in alliance with the Celtic Ulaid (the *Old British* people from whom Ulster gets its name). Nevertheless, under relentless Uí Néill pressure the Ulster leaders were forced to retreat eastwards, and it was possibly this contraction of their territory which occasioned groups within the Northern population to move across the North Channel, in particular the Dál Riata, who settled Argyll and the islands along the western seaboard. It was these settlers, who had been labelled 'Scotti' by the Romans, who bequeathed the name 'Scotland' to their new homeland.

The kings of Dál Riata soon claimed sovereignty over territory on both sides of the North Channel, and from the kings of 'Dalriada' there is a direct link to the kings of Scotland, and thus to William and James themselves. (As grandson and son respectively of Charles I, the two kings were also both directly descended from the Brêton

(Old British) nobility, the progenitors of the House of Stuart, who had 'returned' to Britain with William the Conqueror.)

Apart from the political changes the Celts wrought within Irish society, their most important cultural legacy was the introduction of a vibrant and beautiful language which, when later complemented by an intense outpouring of creativeness, would place Ireland to the forefront of Western European literature. The Ulster emigrants to Scotland were to take this Gaelic language with them and it spread throughout the Highlands and islands – perhaps one of the most remarkable examples of the extent of the interrelationship between the two peoples.

With the arrival of the Christian period Ireland witnessed an upsurge in intense missionary activity which not only spread across the North Channel to Scotland, but was to have a fundamental impact on European history, epitomised by the great missionary journeys of Columbanus.

Another of the great religious figures of Ireland was Columba (Columb-Cille), a prince of the Uí Néill. He became a close friend of Comgall, the Cruthin abbot of the monastery at Bangor – from whence Columbanus was to set forth – even though the political and ethnic rivalries between their respective kinsmen must at times have sorely tested their shared Christianity.

Columba's legend would have us believe that it was these political and ethnic distractions which finally persuaded him to leave Ireland and set up a new community out of sight of its shores. Whatever the reasons, the history of the Church was to be so much the richer, for the community he founded, on the small island of Iona, close to the coast of Argyll, was destined to be the cultural apotheosis of Scotland, and the place some scholars believe the magnificent *Book of Kells* was executed. During this period the cross-fertilisation between Scotland and Ulster was to reach new heights, particularly in the flowering of literary creativeness. As Proinsias Mac Cana wrote: .

> Isolation tends towards stagnation, or at least a circumscribed vision, while conversely intercourse and cultural commerce encourage a greater intellectual curiosity and awareness, a greater readiness to adapt old ways and experiment with new ones. For such intercourse the east-Ulster region was ideally situated. It was a normal landing-place for travellers from northern Britain, which during the sixth and seventh centuries probably presented a more dramatic clash and confluence of cultures than any other

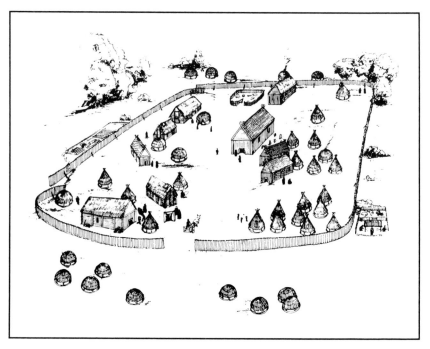

The monastery at Bangor, County Down. Bangor's influence was to be felt not only in nearby Scotland, but further afield in Europe

part of Britain or Ireland; and, in addition, the religious, social and political ties that linked north-eastern Ireland and north-western Britain – particularly in that period – were numerous and close. Archaeologists speak of an 'Irish Sea culture-province' with its western flank in Ireland and its eastern flank in Britain; one might with comparable justification speak of a North Channel culture-province within which obtained a free currency of ideas, literary, intellectual and artistic. [9]

The Gaelic Uí Néill (later synonymous with the O'Neills) had still failed to complete their subjugation of the eastern part of Ulster when that task was accomplished by another body of armed men. In 1169 the first 'Anglo-Normans' arrived on Irish soil, by 'invitation' rather than 'invasion', answering a request by Dermot Mac Murchada, deposed King of Leinster, for assistance in regaining his kingship. In 1177 one of these adventurers, John de Courcy, marched north and captured Downpatrick. The Ulstermen at first strongly opposed this new threat to their independence but increasing raids by the O'Neills forced them to ally with de Courcy. His successor, Hugh de Lacy, was created Earl of Ulster by King John of England.

These first 'Anglo-Normans', however, only retained a tenuous foothold in Ireland, and the Gaelic chiefs continued to resist their presence. Then in 1314 the Scots, under Robert the Bruce, defeated the English at the battle of Bannockburn. O'Neill of Tyrone offered to make Robert's brother Edward King of Ireland, and in May 1315 Edward landed at Larne harbour on the Antrim coast. Following a campaign of devastation Edward Bruce of Scotland was eventually crowned King of Ireland on 1 May 1316, in the presence of a large assembly of Irish and Scottish nobles. He had brought with him 6,000 Scottish mercenaries – the galloglasses – and over the new few centuries the Irish imported a constant stream of these Scots, many of whom were rewarded with land. Edward finally perished in battle near Dundalk in 1318.

One important consequence of the 'Scottish invasion' was that the power of the Earls of Ulster was crushed, and the O'Neills were finally able to fulfil their ultimate ambition of controling the whole of the North. Now at last they could claim to be kings over all of Ulster and the territory of Ulster stretched once again to its ancient boundary of the River Boyne.

The English intensified their efforts at conquest during the reign of Elizabeth I. Despite notable successes for the Gaelic leaders their resistance was finally broken at Kinsale in 1601. Then, on 4 September 1607, after continued harassment by Crown officials, many of Ulster's Gaelic chieftains, including the Earls of Tyrone and Tyrconnell, chose voluntary exile and sailed from Rathmullan for Europe. This act was tantamount to abandoning their people to the mercy of the English, although perhaps for the Irish peasantry the 'Flight of the Earls' was viewed as little more than the replacement of one set of landowners by another, for, as A T Q Stewart pointed out with regard to other Gaelic lords displaced some centuries later: "The lament of the Gael is *their* lament, the poets were *their* poets." [10]

The departure of the Gaelic leaders gave the English government the opportunity to declare their lands forfeit, and some 750,000 acres were confiscated by the Crown. King James I decided to plant settlers in Ulster, hoping that it might prove an effective way of 'civilising' this most rebellious part of Ireland once and for all.

Contemporary woodcut by John Derricke

Gaelic chieftains submit to Elizabeth 1's English Deputy

Sir Arthur Chichester was to be the chief architect of the Plantation in Ulster. However, he was not completely happy with his task. He complained that while good English settlers were being sent to the territories now opening up in the new land of America, most of those coming to Ulster were Scots. Chichester, who bore no real affection for the Irish, looked no more favourably upon the Scots. "He had no special affection for Scotsmen, high or low, gentle or simple, and besides he had spent much of his time and ingenuity ever since his coming to Ireland, in the work of repelling and expelling Islesmen and other Northern Scots from the coasts of Ulster." [11]

Chichester could have saved himself much wasted effort in his attempts to 'repel' such settlers from across the North Channel if he had realised just how much coming and going there had been between Ulster and Scotland throughout history. And as for many of the incoming Scots, F J Bigger was of the opinion: "When the Galloway planters came to Ulster they were only returning to their own lands like emigrants returning home again." [12]

Furthermore, while parts of the Old Earldom which had not been included in the Plantation still spoke English – strongly influenced by Old Norse and Norman French – the planted areas were to receive many Scots settlers who spoke Gaelic.

However, notwithstanding the long-established ties which linked the peoples of Ulster and Scotland, there was a fundamental difference between the new arrivals and the native Irish – the Reformation had swept Scotland and most of the newcomers were Protestants.

The Plantation was not the complete transformation the English Crown had sought. A T Q Stewart writes that, in reality:

> the plantation did not proceed as planned: the Irish were not, as is popularly supposed, driven off the escheated lands wholesale... Without the Irish tenants it is doubtful whether the Scots and English planters would have made even such limited progress as they had by 1641. The great concealed factor in this whole 'British' plantation is the part played by the relatively undisturbed Irish population in building the towns, fortified bawns and planter castles, and in developing the resources of forests, rivers and loughs. In practice, it proved very difficult to persuade English and Scots to take up lands under the plantation scheme, and the evidence that the undertakers did not fulfil their contracts is very extensive. When we remember that the servitors and Irish grantees were actually permitted to take Irish tenants, it becomes clear beyond doubt that a very substantial proportion of the population was not disturbed at all. Modern historical research on the plantation has thrown much light on this continuity of actual population. [10]

The inevitable result was that natives and planters, many of whom already shared a distant kinship, now intermingled still further. Estyn Evans argues that "there was much more intermarriage, with or without the benefit of the clergy, than the conventional histories make allowance for. Many planters became Catholics and many natives became Protestants."[13] Ironically, this constant intermingling of 'Planter' and 'Gael' means that many of today's Protestants and Catholics may not be even be holding – let alone 'defending' – the same allegiances as those held by their forefathers.

However, those Irish who were dispossessed had sufficient cause to harbour a deep-seated resentment. In 1641, with civil unrest in England between Parliamentarians and Royalists, an opportunity was offered to the Catholic Irish to redress the balance, and open rebellion was declared.

Despite the large number of Scots involved in the Plantation and its dispossessions, the Irish rebels had no hesitation acknowledging their close kinship with these settlers, and declared at the beginning of the uprising that the Scottish Presbyterians should be left alone because of their 'Gaelic' origins. Colonel Audeley Mervyn, in a report presented to the House of Commons in June, 1642, stated: "In the infancy of the Rebellion the rebels made open proclamations, upon pain of death, that no Scotchman should be stirred in body, goods or lands, and that they should to this purpose write over the lyntels of their doors that they were Scotchmen, and so destruction might pass over their families." Furthermore, he related that he had read a letter, "sent by two of the rebels, titulary colonels, Colonel Nugent and Colonel O'Gallagher... which was directed to 'Our honourable friends, the gentlemen of the never conquered Scotch nation'." However, the conflict quickly became a sectarian one, and the distinction between Scottish and English settlers was not maintained. The English settlers suffered most, nevertheless, and many thousands lost their lives both in the fighting and in the privations which followed.

Despite a stunning victory at the battle of Benburb by Owen Roe O'Neill and his Catholic Army of Ulster the rebels were hampered by disunity, and resistance was already on the wane when Oliver Cromwell and his Ironside veterans landed in Dublin in 1649, with the intention of restoring this "Bleeding Nation of Ireland to its former happiness and tranquillity", though little of either was to be engendered by his methods.

This then was the situation a few decades before a power struggle in Europe would see the landing in Ireland of a fleeing English king, followed in hot pursuit by his Dutch son-in-law, and their confrontation across the peaceful waters of the River Boyne.

But as Protestants and Catholics in Ireland gathered behind the standards of the two monarchs, this religious difference was the only *real* badge of distinction which could be made between them. What has been detailed in this chapter should have shown clearly that on most other factors – including ethnic background and cultural heritage – the ordinary people who were to spill their blood in the events ahead had far more in common with each other than is generally realised. No longer is the 'Planter' and 'Gael' dichotomy tenable: many of the Scottish 'Planters' clearly shared a close kinship with the native Irish; and as for those who thought of themselves as

'Gaels', their *predominant* inheritance was actually a more ancient one, and one which in all probability they shared with many of those to whom they would soon give battle.

2

— The Rise of the Nation State —

The Battle of the Boyne is so often perceived in the popular imagination as a uniquely 'Irish' event that its European dimension can become totally obscured. How many of Ulster's Orange marchers on their annual celebrations give any thought to the anomaly of Irish Catholics fighting to reinstate a deposed English king who was supported by the king of France, and Irish Protestants fighting for a Dutch prince who was in alliance with the Pope? While in its Irish context the battle has assumed almost overriding importance, on a broader canvas it is revealed as but one part of a complex European power struggle to counter the expansionist ambitions of Louis XIV of France and the arbitrary nature of his feudal monarchy.

As well as obscuring the European dimension to the Battle of the Boyne, many Irishmen somehow imagine that the present-day attributes attached to it – particularly its perceived importance as a victory for a 'British' identity over an 'Irish' identity – accurately reflect the motivations and the certainties of the combatants of that period. However, to assume this would not only be a gross oversimplification, it would also be quite misleading.

Accordingly, just as the previous chapter took a broader historical look at the Irish combatants, the next few chapters will set the scene for the European struggle into which Ireland was inexorably drawn. In so doing, we might begin to see the events of '1690' from a less parochial viewpoint.

This European struggle was but one episode in the long-running saga of conflict as the nation states of Europe competed with each other for dominance. And to understand some of the reasons behind this incessant conflict it is necessary to explore how these states first rose to prominence and the nature of the turmoil they bequeathed to European history.

Most inhabitants of the globe today take for granted the division of the world's surface into different states, each one wielding authority over all those who dwell within its boundaries. Added to this is the popular belief that each state in some way represents, and has always represented, a specific people or 'nation'. However, such assumptions are of relatively modern origin. As J M Roberts pointed out with regard to the Middle Ages: "Hardly any of this would have been intelligible to a European in 1000... No medieval state was national in our sense." [14] (The ethnic tragedy following the break-up of the former Yugoslavia is a prime example of how tenuous is the claim of some 'states' to represent a single 'nation'.)

Following the collapse of the Roman Empire under the weight of 'barbarian' invasions the administrators and proconsuls of the vanquished Empire were replaced by chieftains and warlords:

> All over Europe arose new dominions within which the victors formed a privileged class which imposed [its] will on the working population and led a parasitic life at their expense. The victorious intruders partitioned large sections of the conquered territory among themselves and made the inhabitants pay tribute... Meanwhile the chiefs and army leaders claimed ever greater prerogatives, which logically grew to royal powers. [15]

The impact upon the settled populations of Europe of these new 'intruders' produced a complex intermingling of peoples and cultures. When the Anglo-Saxons arrived in Britain, for example – in numbers which are not believed to have exceeded 25,000, while the already established Romano-British population has been variously estimated at between one and four million – there is no evidence of any widespread massacre of the indigenous population, but rather the peaceful assimilation of the different cultures, which by the 7th century took on the umbrella term of 'Saxon' or 'English', dominated by an Anglo-Saxon élite. [16]

Another 'intrusion' was that of the Normans into northern France, especially appropriate to our study, as the 'Anglo-Norman' conquest of Ireland was to have such a fundamental impact upon the history of this island and its people.

> The long coastline of north-west France drifts into a mixed countryside of fertile pastures, woodlands and gentle hills. This was a seductive landscape to the marauding Vikings of the 9th and 10th centuries. They ravaged towns and monasteries with such freedom that the French king Charles the Simple made a

historic deal with one of the invaders, a Viking warlord named Rollo. In AD 911 he offered the warrior large tracts of land at the mouth of the Seine as a duchy, clearly hoping that the outlander would screen his realm from further Viking incursions.

The gamble worked. Rollo and his son not only held but expanded the original land grant, which acted as the required buffer. In due course the Vikings intermarried with the local population and adopted French as their tongue. Through linguistic contraction, the Norsemen, or Northmen, came to be known as Normans. And their duchy was Normandy. [17]

As the 'Irish' still hold the 'English' to blame for the 'Anglo-Norman' invasion, it is worth pointing out that the 'English' themselves were not very pleased when these Normans eventually arrived on *their* soil. An English chronicler in 1137 had bemoaned: "And they filled the land full of castles; and when the castles were made they filled them with devils and evil men." Lewis Warren wrote:

> The English suffered more from the Normans than the Irish ever did. In Domesday Book there is no trace of the great families which had ruled England before 1066; in Ireland the leading families whose names are familiar from long before the Normans arrived are still there four hundred years later. [18]

Under the first surge of the 'barbarians' not only had the Roman system of government collapsed but the Christian church had been brought close to disintegration. Yet it was into this chaos that the Irish were to make their most significant contribution to European history. Ireland had been largely unaffected by the barbarian invasions, just as it had been only indirectly touched by Roman civilisation, with the result that the Church had survived intact and its traditions of learning had continued unimpaired.

Of the many Irish monasteries which emerged, one of the most influential was that of Bangor, on the coast of present-day County Down. Bangor, where vernacular Gaelic was influenced by original native British and contemporary Latin, became the central focus of an east Ulster region credited with being "the cradle of written Irish literature",[9] and one of the most unique documents produced there – the seventh century manuscript known as the 'Bangor Antiphonary' – differs in wording from all other know versions, and is, in substance, the original Creed of Nicaea.

In 589 a small band of men set out from Bangor on what was to become one of the great missionary journeys of history. Led by Columbanus and Gall the group founded monasteries wherever they travelled, which in turn became the inspiration for countless others.

These and other Irish monasteries reintroduced the [Christian] faith and brought with them their libraries, both classical and Christian, which had remained safe in Ireland during the migration period. The influence of the Irish on European culture can hardly be overemphasized. [19]

Pope Pius XI has said, "The more light that is shed by scholars in the period known as the Middle Ages the clearer it becomes that it was thanks to the initiative and labours of Columbanus that the rebirth of Christian virtue and civilisation over a great part of Gaul, Germany and Italy took place." [20]

Indeed, in that period when civil administrations were weak, it was the Church which often acted as the great unifying factor right across Europe.

Another civilising force was also working patiently to prevent the disintegration of European society – the ordinary people. Everywhere men and women rebelled against the tyranny of the nobles and the bishops, and fought for a readjustment of the conditions of their social life. As Rudolf Rocker explained:

...the victorious communities won their 'charters' and created their city constitutions in which the new legal status found expression. But even where the communities were not strong enough to achieve full independence they forced the ruling power to far-reaching concessions. Thus evolved from the tenth to the fifteenth century that great epoch of the free cities and of federalism whereby European culture was preserved from total submersion and the political influence of the arising royalty was for a long time confined to the non-urban country.

In that great period of federalism... all countries were covered by a close net of fraternal associations, trade guilds, church parishes, county associations, city confederations, and countless other alliances arising from free agreement. The medieval community was in all fields of its rich social and vital activities arranged according to social, not governmental, considerations.[15]

Hence 'Europeans' of that era, as well as being the product of a complex intermingling of peoples and cultures, viewed their communal rights and obligations as stemming from custom and tradition, rather than from any specifically 'national' institutions.

As a consequence, Europe's citizenry in general lacked our modern concept of the 'nation' and 'national consciousness' – which in turn makes that epoch quite incomprehensible to many today.

However, an intricate web of political and commercial forces – often in competition – was at work within Europe which would fundamentally change all that. Of primary importance, from the 13th century onwards, was the tendency for *kings* in almost every part of Europe to consolidate their power: "In all the kingdoms royal power grew at the expense of the competing institutions, whether nobility, parliaments, free cities, or clergy, and almost everywhere the eclipse of the medieval representative system was permanent."[21] Also, there was a gradual increase in the power of commercial capital, due in the main to the lands opened up by the Great Age of Discovery. As G H Sabine pointed out:

> For the first time since the Roman Empire European society included a considerable class of men who had both money and enterprise. For obvious reasons this class was the natural enemy of the nobility and of all the divisions and disorders which they fostered. Their interests were on the side of 'strong' government both at home and abroad, and hence their natural political alliance was with the king. For the time being they were content to see his power increase at the expense of all the checks and limitations which had surrounded medieval monarchy... From every point of view the bourgeoisie saw its advantage in concentrating military power and the administration of justice as much as possible in the hands of the king. [21]

The institution which most rivalled the growing power of royalty was the Church, and the two forces were frequently in conflict. The Church drained money from each country to finance the pope's political ambitions, and there was increasing opposition to its external interference in the affairs of each kingdom.

The Church itself was responsible for much of its own problems. The Great Schism – in which two and sometimes three rival popes resorted to every type of invective and political chicanery against each other – did much to destroy the popular respect in which the papal office had previously been held. Absenteeism and corruption were rife among the clergy, the immoral behaviour of many of them doing much to discredit the Church in the eyes of laymen. "It was the conjuncture of a spiritually bankrupt yet materially acquisitive church at a time of heightened religious awareness which explains why a religious revolution occurred in the 16th century." [22]

When the Protestant Reformation finally provided a focus for the widespread disillusionment with the Church, it struck a sympathetic chord not only among many sections of the disillusioned populace, but among some of the rulers of the emerging nation states, whose interests would be served by any political weakening of the Church.

Paradoxically the reform movement led to the strengthening of secular power. The reformers found themselves dependent on royal power to coerce the Papacy, and the 'divine right of kings' became almost an official philosophy for Lutherans and Anglicans. The break with Rome allowed the northern princes to increase their own authority, as well as providing them with the opportunity to seize church estates and transfer the rich returns into their own treasuries.

The reform movement, however, was augmented by another powerful force – the revolutionary masses, who in rural areas in particular were sorely oppressed by serfdom. The peasantry directed their attacks not just against the failures and abuses of the Church, but at the whole structure of society. In Northern Italy, Flanders, France, England, Germany and Bohemia, from the 13th to the 16th century, peasant revolts sought to abolish social inequalities and the privileges of the rich.

> [These] peasant revolts were feared and hated by the rising bourgeoisie of the sixteenth century more fiercely and more nervously than similar proletarian disturbances of a later day. They were suppressed with savage cruelty, which received the blessing of both Luther and Calvin. Not for nothing did monarchy receive the support of the growing middle class, but for this reason also the religious reformers were thrown bodily into the arms of the princes. Thus the Reformation joined with economic forces already in existence to make royal government, invested with absolute power at home and with a free hand abroad, the typical form of European state. [21]

Luther in particular expressed little sympathy with, or respect for, the masses of mankind:

> The princes of this world are gods, the common people are Satan, through whom God sometimes does what at other times he does directly through Satan, that is, makes rebellion as a punishment for the people's sins. I would rather suffer a prince doing wrong than a people doing right... It is in no wise proper

29

for anyone who would be a Christian to set himself up against his government, whether it acts justly or unjustly. There are no better works than to obey and serve all those who are set over us as superiors. For this reason also disobedience is a greater sin than murder, unchastity, theft, and dishonesty, and all that these may include. [23]

One of the leaders of the peasant insurrection in Germany, Thomas Müntzer, accused the princes of using the Law of God – specifically the commandment 'thou shalt not steal' – to protect the property which they themselves had appropriated, and he castigated Luther for supporting them: "The wretched flatterer is silent... about the origin of all theft... Look, the seed-grounds of usury and theft and robbery are our lords and princes, they take all creatures as their property: the fish in the water, the birds in the air, the plants on the ground have all got to be theirs." [24]

In his vehement pamphlet *Against the Murdering, Thieving Hordes of Peasants* Luther outlined to the princes his violent remedy for the proponents of such radical beliefs. Ultimately, the peasant risings were savagely suppressed, and according to Rudolf Rocker:

> In the other countries, too, Protestantism pursued the same ends; everywhere it betrayed the people and made of the Reformation an affair of the princes and the privileged sections of society... Protestantism had freed the conscience of man from the guardianship of the church only to barter it to the state. [15]

As if the merciless defeat of the peasantry was not enough, bloody wars of religion were soon to devastate Europe and inflict untold misery upon its citizens. The intensifying struggle for power between princes and kings, priests and reformers, barons and merchants, enveloped the lives of ordinary people right across the continent. And as an ever-present backdrop the new nation states of Europe were consolidating and the peasantry of Europe were being marshalled to make war upon each other in defence of gradually coalescing concepts of 'national interest' and 'national identity'.

> It was not the people who brought about this new condition, for no inner necessity drove them to this division, nor could they derive any benefit from it. The national state is the definite result of the will to temporal power, which in pursuit of its purposes had found a powerful support in commercial capital, which needed its help. The princes imposed their will on the people and resorted to all sorts of tricks to keep them compliant,

so that later it appeared as if the division of Christendom into nations had originated with the people themselves, whereas actually they were but the unconscious tools of the special interests of the princes. [15]

We will never know the full story of the cost in lives and suffering paid by the inhabitants of Europe during the emergence of the nation states – the writing of 'history' has always been more concerned with the doings of kings, generals and popes, a bias reinforced by the assumption that the growth of strong states was an inevitable part of Mankind's efforts to create 'civilisation' out of chaos. Yet, the evidence reveals another side to this story – for example, the number of battles engaged in by the principal European powers in modern times shows an unmistakeable trend: 87 battles in the 16th century, 239 in the 17th century, 781 in the 18th century.[25] Erich Fromm, in his psychological analysis of 'human destructiveness', drew the following conclusion: "[Major] wars in modern times and most wars between the states of antiquity were not caused by dammed-up aggression, but by instrumental aggression of the military and political élites... the number and intensity of wars has risen with the development of technical civilisation; it is highest among the powerful states with a strong government and lowest among primitive man without permanent chieftainship." [26]

Alongside the endeavours of the masses to pursue their everyday lives as best they could despite the frequent depredations inflicted upon them by the ambitions of their rulers must be added the efforts of all those individuals who really did contribute to the betterment of humanity: the genuinely caring priests who tried to change the Church from within; the great Protestant reformers such as John Knox and the Scots Worthies who displayed a truly social commitment; and the host of craftsmen, sculptors, writers, scientists, and musicians who bequeathed to Europe a unique cultural legacy.

These communal endeavours and creative individual efforts were often as not hindered rather than advanced by the consolidation of religious and secular power. Despite the seemingly irreconcilable differences between one prince and another, one king and another, between Catholicism and Protestantism, one new 'state' and another, these forces often had more in common with each other than with the spontaneous action of the masses or the radical ideals of free-thinkers. This is nowhere better exemplified than with the story of Michael Servetus.

Michael Servetus (Miguel Serveto of Navarre) was born in Spain in 1511. Although he had a distinguished career as a medical practitioner – and is credited with discovering the pulmonary circulation of the blood – it was on philosophical matters than he focused his speculative, daring and iconoclastic genius.

He believed that he possessed the power, and had received a commission, to remodel all knowledge, and establish the world on a new basis. The more fundamental doctrines of Christianity became the object of his settled dislike... Romanism he had renounced in his youth, but neither did the Reformation satisfy his grand ideal. Christianity, he held, had been lost at an early age, if indeed it had ever been fully promulgated to the world. Servetus undertook to restore and re-institute it. [27]

Servetus on his way to execution

He denied the divinity of Christ, his beliefs akin to pantheism which held that there was no personal Deity – God was manifest in all parts of the material universe – and he came close to the views of the Anabaptists, who believed that infants were unaware of good and evil and therefore not punishable for sin. He sent Calvin a manuscript on his ideas, but the latter was horrified at what he regarded as heresy, and, in a letter to a colleague, mentioned Servetus's request to come to Geneva: "I am unwilling to pledge my word for his safety, for if he shall come, I will never permit him to depart alive, provided my authority be of any avail."

The same manuscript led to Servetus's arrest by the Roman Catholic Inquisition, and although he managed to escape he was condemned in his absence to be "burned alive, at a slow fire, till his body be reduced to a cinder". During the trial the Catholic authorities were aided by evidence furnished by Calvin. Yet it was to Calvin's Geneva that Servetus fled, in retrospect an unwise decision, for upon arrival Calvin reported his presence to the authorities and had him arrested. At his trial it was evident that the judges considered his views to be not just heretical, but seditious, and the roots of political authority no less than religious authority could, they believed, be threatened by such sedition. And with the Protestant judges in Geneva being just as concerned with upholding the principle of 'authority' as those of the Catholic Inquisition, it was the Calvinists who in the end sent Servetus to his death – they too ordaining that his fate was to be burned alive, his heretical treatise *Restitutio Christianismi* bound to his side.

The efforts of such individuals must have seemed predestined to failure when set in opposition to the growing and all-embracing power of religious and secular authority now being consolidated in the emerging nation states. One of these states in particular was to stamp itself formidably upon the map of Europe, and it is to the religious and political history of that country – France – that we now turn.

3

— French Ambitions —

The culture, language, literature and philosophical and political ideas of the people of France have assured their nation a prominent place in European and world history. It was the Romans who first forged a sense of unity among the various tribal kingdoms within the area known as Gaul, and although much of the pre-Roman culture was destroyed in the process, the Roman occupation bequeathed towns, roads, theatres and aqueducts as well as an extensive system of administration. The Roman Empire finally collapsed under the twin pressures of internal decline and invasion by Germanic tribes. Among these invaders one group in particular – the Franks – proved to be the most successful. They settled in northern Gaul and adapted a variety of Latin which ultimately became French. These Franks, who also adopted Christianity, created the nucleus of modern France.

Their greatest king, Charlemagne, extended Frankish territory well beyond the confines of Gaul, establishing an empire which covered most of western Europe by the time of his death in 814. "Charlemagne's court at Aachen became a brilliant centre of European culture, fostering a flowering of art and learning so spectacular that it has been called the Carolingian Renaissance." [17] Charlemagne was to build one of his most famous foundations – the Monastery of St Gall – near the spot where Gall, Columbanus's travelling companion from Bangor, had lived the austere life of a hermit. A modern monastery now stands there today, of which John Romer has written:

> The monastery... has in its library beautiful Irish manuscripts made by some of these travelling scholars. The library has also preserved a fine plan of Charlemagne's monastery with its sties and stables, its sheepfolds and fowl houses, threshing floors and market gardens... As well as this farm neatly laid out in a great rectangle around the central church, the monastery of St Gall had a hostel and a kitchen for its guests, schools and accommodation for the abbot and his monks, a doctor's clinic, and infirmary and a

A drawing of St Gall in the 16th century

cemetery. Such settlements formed the high culture of Europe in the reign of Charlemagne. [28]

In 800, Pope Leo III revived an old title and crowned Charlemagne 'Emperor of the Roman Empire in the West'. This 'Holy Roman Empire' was to survive up to the 19th century, although it was to be frequently at odds with the very papacy which created it. After Charlemagne's death the Empire began to break up, and at the Treaty of Verdun in 843 his grandsons agreed to its division, with only that area now roughly corresponding to the territory of Germany retaining the title of Holy Roman Empire.

Many regions now regarded as quintessentially 'French' were at one time independent territories, none more so than Normandy, which had greatly consolidated since its origin as a Viking settlement. Although William, Duke of Normandy (later to become known as William 'the Conqueror') repulsed two 'French' invasions, it was to be across the English Channel that he was to greatly extend Norman territory, following his victory at the Battle of Hastings in 1066. Such a powerful domain straddling the Channel inevitably brought English

35

interests into constant conflict with those of France. This situation was greatly exacerbated when Henry II of England, through marriage, was able to gain further large tracts of western France, so that English dominions now stretched from the Channel to the Pyrenees.

In those parts of France not claimed by England, the king of France wielded less power than the various virtually autonomous regions, many of which – just like Normandy – reflected separate regional identities which had resulted from earlier invasions – for example, the Visigoths in Aquitaine and the Burgundians in Burgundy. However, between 1000 and 1500 the power of the French kings gradually consolidated, a more centralised administration was developed, and 'Francia' expanded to incorporate more and more of the territory which today makes up modern France. The undermining of the English hold on western France was to be a constant objective of French 'foreign' policy. Furthermore, a new sense of nationhood was nurtured in each country as a direct consequence of their quarrels with one another. One significant episode in the struggle between the two countries was the Hundred Years' War. As J M Roberts has pointed out:

> The Hundred Years' War was also indirectly important to the French monarchy because it did something to check feudal fragmentation and moved Frenchman about, breaking down in some degree the barriers between Picard and Gascon, Norman and French... The other important result was England's defeat in the longer run; her territorial connection with France was virtually at an end by 1500 (though in the eighteenth century George III was still entitled 'King of France'). England became almost an island again. After 1453 French kings could push forward with the consolidation of their state undisturbed by the obscure claims of England's rulers from which the wars had sprung. They could settle down to establish their sovereignty over their rebellious magnates at their leisure. In each country, war in the long run strengthened the state. [14]

France emerged from the Middle Ages a rich and powerful state, under the centralised authority of an absolute monarch. Yet the position of the monarchy remained unstable, having to contend with rival factions among the nobility who vied with each other for influence and power. The rise of Protestantism was to complicate matters further. The intense hostility engendered all over Europe between the rival branches of Christianity was reflected in the competition for power and influence among the leading families of the French nobility – with the result that France was to experience thirty years of religious wars.

The political and religious tensions among the nobility, heightened by numerous disputes around the country, as Protestants illegally seized churches and Catholics fought to recover them, drifted inexorably towards civil war. Between the warring factions stood that remarkable woman, Catherine de' Medici, mother of the king then reigning and the one to follow. Her main concern was to preserve the unity of France, and she considered that object was best served by keeping Catholicism and Protestantism in balance. "Her own attitude to religion was ambiguous, but she well realised its importance to others, and to herself as a factor in temporal politics... She was the perfect Renaissance princess according to the Machiavellian ideal: not gratuitously cruel, but ruthless when occasion seemed to demand it." [29]

Even though Catholics were still the majority in France, the leading Huguenots began to gain some of the highest offices of state through diplomacy and royal favour. By 1560 a distinctive religious geography of Protestantism was emerging in the country, with some 2,150 Huguenot communities. Perhaps as much as half of the nobility and a third of the bourgeoisie had become Protestant.[30] In 1570 as well as being granted liberty of opinion and worship, the Huguenots were allowed control of four well-defended towns, of which the most important was the large port of La Rochelle. The king now began to favour some of his Huguenot advisors, even to the exclusion of his mother. Not only was the Catholic nobility extremely troubled by this trend but the inhabitants of Paris were seething. The situation reached a crisis on 18 August 1572 when Catherine's daughter Margaret married Henry of Bourbon, King of Navarre – and a Protestant. The spectre of the throne of France being occupied by a Protestant haunted the Catholic parties, especially when they considered what little influence their co-religionists in England had retained when that country converted to Protestantism.

In an attempt to prevent the situation deteriorating further, Catherine and leading members of the Catholic nobility – even the king himself, after he was finally persuaded – set in motion the events which have become notorious as the Massacre of St Bartholomew's Eve, during which, on 24 August 1572, Catholics massacred 2,700 Huguenots in Paris and more than 20,000 in the provinces.

The harbour of La Rochelle

Although there was to be no ongoing persecution following the massacre – indeed, the Huguenots grew stronger in their determination – French Catholic fears appeared to be confirmed when, following the king's death, Henry of Navarre became Henry IV of France. However, four years of bitter fighting followed and Henry's kingship was only recognised by French Catholics when he converted to Catholicism – "Paris is worth a Mass", he is reputed to have said. His persistent Huguenot countrymen, however, secured from him the Edict of Nantes in 1598, a remarkably tolerant piece of legislation for the time. Through it the Huguenots received financial support from the state to maintain their clergy, widespread freedom of worship, and liberty to hold public office and attend colleges and academies. Although this tolerance met with opposition from the Catholic clergy, it marked the end of the Wars of Religion and seemed to open up for France a new period of unity.

The two 17th century rulers of France, Louis XIII and Louis XIV, concerned themselves with strengthening the centralised state as personified in the person of the king – "L'état c'est moi" as Louis XIV would describe it – and securing the external borders of the realm. Despite the Edict of Nantes – and also because of it – hostility still divided the religious protagonists. In 1621, during a period of heightened suspicion and harassment, the Protestants of La Rochelle held an assembly at which they came near to declaring independence.

> They claimed the full benefit of the Edict of Nantes, which seemed to the court to be the establishment of a republic in the heart of the monarchy. They divided their 700 congregations throughout France into eight circles, after the German fashion, thus indicating a tendency towards decentralisation, which must be offensive to the court and the general body of French people; they arranged their own levies of men and money, and in fact went far towards the full organisation of what they styled 'the republic of the Reformed churches of France and Béarn.' [31]

To the royal court all this was anathema and in 1627 Louis XIII's minister, Richelieu, deciding that autonomous fortresses were a threat to the security of the kingdom, attacked and took La Rochelle, finally neutralising this major military threat posed by French Protestants. Out of a population of 25,000 at least 10,000 died rather than surrender.

Louis XIV, who, as we shall see shortly, was to deal the French Huguenots an even deadlier blow than his predecessor, consolidated the power and prestige of France and emerged as the greatest ruler in Europe, becoming known as the 'Sun King' because of the opulence and splendour of his court. When diplomacy failed to increase France's wealth and territory, he had at his command a well trained professional army of some 200,000 men to carry out his ambitions through military means.

> The great fact of the new age in Europe was the advance of French arms and influence across the continent. The decadence of Spain, and the

Cardinal Richelieu

39

failure of Germany and Italy to produce one formidable power among the innumerable States into which their vast territories were divided, left the way open for the ambition of France. Her unity and internal organisation had been perfected by Cardinals Richelieu and Mazarin, and bequeathed by them to Louis XIV and the brilliant group of soldiers and statesmen who served him in his youth. In the ten years since the death of Cromwell the danger had become apparent to all the world. The States of Europe, Catholic as well as Protestant, were in panic, but their inefficiency, selfishness, and mutual jealousy prevented their union for self-defence before William of Orange arose to marshal them. [32]

However, even mighty nations can be humbled, as France was to discover in 1672 when Louis embarked on a war which he must have supposed would result in speedy victory – against the small Republic of Holland.

4

— Enter the Dutch —

Holland wielded an influence upon European affairs at that time
which belied its small size. Historian G M Trevelyan has summarised
its significance:

> Amid the effete monarchies and princedoms of feudal Europe,
> morally and materially exhausted by the Thirty Years' War, the
> only hope of resistance to France lay in the little Republic of
> merchants, Holland poised between the sand-banks and the sea.
> Enriched by its eastern colonies, its world-wide commerce, and
> its open door for refugees of all races and beliefs, the home of
> Grotius, Descartes, and Spinoza, of Rembrandt and Vermeer, led
> the world in philosophy, learning, finance, painting, gardening,
> scientific agriculture, and many other of the arts and crafts that
> liberate and adorn the life of man. Holland was a rival influence
> to France in Europe, and stood on this height without the parade
> of King, noble, or prelate. Her first magistrate, the admired De
> Witt, kept a single servant in his house and walked unattended
> through the streets.[32]

The ancestors of the modern Dutch were two Germanic tribes, the
Batavians and the Frisians. Their territory eventually became
incorporated into Charlemagne's Empire, Charlemagne himself
sometimes keeping his court at Nijmegen on the River Waal.

Although the Empire broke up after Charlemagne's death into its
various kingdoms, the idea of a Holy Roman Empire was revived,
and while in theory the Emperor was chosen for life from among the
rulers of central Europe, in practice the title became hereditary in
one family – the Hapsburgs of Austria. The Hapsburgs gradually
extended their dominions through marriages with the Spanish and
other royal families and by the end of the 15th century their own
hereditary domains were dotted haphazardly over much of Europe,
and included present-day Holland and Belgium.

When Charles V became Emperor in 1519, he had already

Repulse of the Spanish

succeeded his father Philip as Duke of Burgundy in 1509, and his grandfather Ferdinand as King of Aragon and of Castille in 1516. Apart from these dynastic connections, the Empire had no real geographical logic to it, and the difficulties of communication between the disparate parts made it almost impossible to govern. The burden proved too much for Charles and he eventually abdicated, handing control of The Netherlands and Spain to his son Philip, and control of Austria, Bohemia and Hungary to his brother Ferdinand.

Charles had been born and reared in the Netherlands, and although he was a Catholic, he had not been prepared to have the Dutch Protestants of his homeland subjected to the horrors of the Inquisition. Philip, however, had no such scruples, and his repressive policies finally provoked the Dutch into rebellion. After a war which lasted eighty years the former Spanish possession was divided into the independent Dutch Republic in the north and the 'obedient' provinces of the south (which later became Belgium).

A new state had emerged in Europe, unique in its constitution, social structure and economy. It was a country in which a new class was in control – a mercantile republic had successfully revolted against the absolute monarchy which typified the other states of Europe. "In economic and financial matters the Dutch were pre-eminent. Amsterdam had the world's first stock-exchange as far back as 1602. The Bank of Amsterdam was set up in 1609, long before the Bank of England. State lotteries and the concept of 'excise' duties were similarly first introduced in the Netherlands." [33]

Charles Wilson has charted the extent of Dutch influence:

> Almost every country in Europe profited from Dutch immigration. From London to Rome and Danzig to Warsaw, Dutch settlers used their engineering skills to clear swamps and marshes and to build dams, locks and canals, water works and pumping systems. Colbert employed Dutchmen in Bordeaux to reclaim land and build textile factories, and in Sweden Dutch immigrants negotiated contracts with the crown that gave them a virtual monopoly of iron and copper mining, the manufacture of munitions, the cutting of timber and the export of tar, hemp and rope.
>
> The 'new drapery' – carried by Belgian emigrants from Ypres to Leyden, and then to Norwich and Colchester – revolutionised Europe's textile trade, replacing old, heavy, expensive cloths with bright, light, cheaper textiles. Antwerp silk weavers and linen bleachers carried their skills to Amsterdam and Haarlem... In ensuing decades, Dutch bankers helped to shape the structure and finance of the Bank of England... In their heyday, Dutch capital, Dutch enterprise and Dutch technology – all by-products of the Dutch revolt – served as a powerful driving force, propelling a predominantly agrarian, semifeudal Europe toward industrial revolution and socio-economic modernity. [34]

As well as their mercantile expertise the Dutch established themselves as a formidable naval power. Through the Dutch East India Company they had their own empire in the East, and in America they founded New Amsterdam, later to become New York, from which they traded with and evangelised the Mohawk people. Their prowess at sea brought them into competition with England and in the course of a succession of naval wars between the two countries the Dutch sailed up the Medway, a tributary of the Thames, and burnt or carried off some of England's best ships.

It was therefore not difficult for Louis XIV in 1670 to forge an alliance with England – the treaty of Dover – by which the two powers were to invade Holland, destroy its commercial power and

View of Amsterdam

partition the country. Louis, using his wife's Spanish connection as a pretext – she was the daughter of Philip IV of Spain by that monarch's first marriage – demanded the cession of certain of the Spanish provinces in the Low Countries and invaded in 1672.

But the French had reckoned without the stubbornness of the Dutch. The small nation was ostensibly a republic but there was still popular support for the old princedom, the House of Orange, then represented by William of Orange, who was also the King of England's nephew. And when the French invaded it was the House of Orange around which the populace rallied, not the Republic. The leading republicans, the De Witts, were murdered, the Republic overthrown, and Holland was once again united under the House of Orange. Dutch resilience was now to prove itself:

> [They] cut the dykes, letting the water of the canalized rivers flow over the low meadows, and at the sacrifice of their drowned property brought the French armies to a standstill. Meanwhile their seamen at Solebay more than held their own against the

44

united fleets of England and France, and William's genius for diplomacy enabled him to build in haste the first of his many European coalitions against Louis. [32]

Opinion in England eventually came round to believe that the war was not really one between England and Holland for naval supremacy, but part of Louis XIV's design for European conquest, and Parliament withdrew England from the war. There were suspicions within the Anglican Cavalier Parliament that England's own king, Charles II, was an accomplice to this design, a suspicion reinforced when it was learned with alarm that the heir to the throne, Charles's brother James, had become a Roman Catholic. In fact, in a secret part of the Treaty of Dover, Louis had promised Charles, who was himself half-French in blood and breeding, a large subsidy to continue the war with Holland. A reaction took place against the king, and, alarmed by it, he spent the rest of his reign working in closer alliance with Parliament. As for the war in Holland, the Dutch prevailed and France was forced to make peace in 1678.

Louis himself admitted a grudging admiration for his Dutch adversaries: "The resolution to put the entire country under the water was a bit violent; but what will one not do to prevent the domination of a foreigner? I cannot help admiring and praising the zeal and fortitude of those who broke off the negotiations [to accept his terms] ... even though their advice, so salutary for their fatherland, brought great prejudice to my service." [35]

However, Louis was not to be diverted from his territorial and political ambitions and it would not be long before he and his adversary William of Orange confronted each other again over the destiny of Europe.

Louis XIV revokes the Edict of Nantes

5

— Louis chooses Intolerance —

On 18 October 1685 Louis XIV set his name to a document which was but the final confirmation of a fundamental change in France's domestic policy, one which was to have far-reaching consequences not only for France but for the history of Europe. John Laurence Carr has admirably depicted the scene:

> In a hall on the first floor of the palace of Fontainebleau a glittering assembly had been gathered... At the end opposite the colonnaded entrance and the arched windows, which looked down into the Cour Ovale, could be seen the two-tier dais, surmounted by the vast canopy covering the throne, and a cushion for the royal feet. Here was Louis XIV of France appropriately robed for the important ceremony about to take place and wearing the brilliant state crown. Behind him were three or four pages and – significantly, because the thorny and dangerous subject of religion was under discussion – a number of guards armed with pikes. To his left were gentleman-ushers ready to respond to his slightest behest. Around [a table a mere four yards from the royal dais] were seated up to fifty important dignitaries – ministers of the crown, men of the cloth, high-ranking officers of French legal bodies and the like. Tightly packed between this central group and the [rich Gobelins tapestries arrayed on the distant walls] were two hundred men of secondary importance, including clerics from provincial dioceses invited to Fontainebleau to witness the historic transformation that was being enacted beneath the sparkling chandeliers. [36]

Louis was revoking the Edict of Nantes, promulgated in 1598 by Henry IV, which had guaranteed freedom of religion to the Protestants of France.

The generous and enlightened terms of the original Edict had not met with widespread approval in France. Many leading Catholics felt that the promises made to the Protestants went too far and should only be seen as a temporary expedient. In the reign of Louis XIII Catholic Church leaders had constantly urged the monarch to do all he could to make life difficult for those who professed or promoted the Protestant faith. Events in the small Pyrenean territory of Béarn highlighted the rigor with which the king applied himself to this task. Despite the majority of Béarn's citizens being Protestant a decree was issued in 1617 which handed over all their ecclesiastical property to the Catholic clergy. When all classes in the territory united against this tyranny soldiers were sent in to ensure compliance and violence was directed against the populace and their churches.

The culmination of these events was, as we have already seen, the taking of the Protestant stronghold of La Rochelle by royal forces. Upon the city's fall its ancient privileges were annulled and the Catholic religion re-established, Pope Urban VIII giving his blessing with a *Te Deum* in Rome.

Louis XIV was now to pursue his predecessor's work with a vengeance. He was firmly convinced that Protestantism weakened France and must be eradicated. Further, he considered the Edict of Nantes to have been a grave error. The Catholic Church, using the payments they made to the State treasury as added leverage, urged him to interpret the Edict more rigorously. The Edict had not stated specifically that the Protestants could build churches, so those built since were ordered to be demolished. If title deeds could not be produced, or had gone missing through time, it provided an excuse for a church to be suppressed. Untold numbers of churches were pulled down, schools closed, and charitable establishments confiscated by the Catholic Church. Protestants were increasingly barred from taking up various occupations. Spies sat in on sermons, and if the pastor spoke disparagingly of the Virgin he was indicted for blasphemy.

A new stage began with the *dragonnades* – the forced billeting of soldiers in Protestant households. The number of soldiers allotted to each family ranged from four to ten. Short of actually killing the family members, it was made clear to the soldiers that they could act in any way they wished – and they cruelly proceeded to do just that, inflicting untold suffering and despair upon the Protestant population. Thousands of Protestants now began to flee the country, while many more, unable to live under the terror, put their names forward for conversion. The *dragonnades* had begun in the province of Poitou but were deemed so successful that they were extended to

The Flight of the French Huguenots

all the provinces of Southern France, including the district of Orange, William's principality. Everywhere Protestants were forced to flee into the forests or the mountains, where many were tracked down by the soldiers and brutally murdered. Churches which had been spared up to then were now demolished.

In the face of this Terror the conversion rate soared, including twenty thousand in Béarn, and sixty thousand in the two dioceses of Nîmes and Montpellier. Pope Innocent XI, who was opposed to forced conversions, condemned Louis's actions. The Edict of Nantes may still have been in place, but it was now a meaningless piece of paper – it only remained for the final act to be played out, and on 18 October Louis signed the Revocation.

> On the 22nd of October the Act was registered and on the same day the Protestants were notified by a public spectacle that its execution had commenced. The great Church of Charenton, in the neighbourhood of Paris, built by the celebrated architect Jacques Debrosse, and capable of containing 14,000 persons, was razed to the ground. The first blow was dealt the detested structure by two Government commissioners; then a mob of some hundred threw themselves upon it, with pickaxes and levers; in five days not a trace of the colossal fabric was to be seen, and a cross twenty feet high, adorned with the royal arms, rose in triumph over the demolished edifice. [27]

The Revocation of the Edict of Nantes suppressed all the privileges granted to the Huguenots, inhibited the exercise of the Protestant religion, enjoined the banishment of all its ministers within 15 days, held out rewards for converts, and prohibited keeping schools, or bringing up children, in any but the Catholic religion. Dragoons were sent into Languedoc, Dauphine and Provence to enforce the decree, and a torrent of pillagings, outrages and murders swept over France. It has been estimated that some half-million Huguenots fled France throughout the whole period of persecution. They migrated mostly to the British Isles, Holland and Germany, and brought with them their arts, industry and resentment.

The nobility were delighted with their monarch, the Church ecstatic:

> Touched by so many marvels let us expand our hearts in praises of the piety of Louis. Let our acclamations ascend to the skies, and let us say to this new Constantine, this new Theodosius, this new Marcian, this new Charlemagne... 'You have strengthened

faith, you have exterminated heretics, it is a work worthy of your reign, whose proper character it is. Thanks to you, heresy is no more.' [27]

In reality, it was one of Louis's greatest mistakes. All of Europe could now see the totalitarian nature of France and her monarch, and within a few years Protestant *and* Catholic states were to unite under the leadership of William of Orange to counter French territorial and political ambitions.

6

— Vanity and Power —

Louis XIV was an 'absolute' ruler in every sense of the word. On the death of Cardinal Mazarin, who had nurtured and coached the king through the early years of his reign, Louis made it perfectly clear to his Chancellor, ministers and secretaries of state just who was in charge of France:

> Sir, ... up to the present time, I have been content to leave the governing of my affairs in the hands of the late Cardinal Mazarin. However, the time has now come for me to take over the reins of government myself. You will kindly assist my by giving me the benefit of your advice, *when I ask you for it...* From now on, Mr Chancellor, you will not make any decision or sign any paper except on my orders and not before having discussed the matter with me, unless, of course, you are brought these orders directly from me by one of my secretaries of state. As for you, sirs, as my secretaries of state, I forbid you to sign anything at all, not even a safe-conduct pass or a passport, without my prior approval.

Not just matters of government, but almost all aspects of life in France were subject to Louis's will and authority. As Philippe Erlanger has pointed out:

Cardinal Mazarin

52

He controlled everything – from the order of precedence at court to troop movements and theological controversies. Nothing – from an important marriage to the building of a road – could be arranged without his approval... Louis created an excellent intelligence service and founded the modern police force, but his authority was never based on a system of police terror. He succeeded in stifling the various factions, destroying the parties and wiping out ideological divisions with the general approval of the people and without resorting to violence." [37]

Louis dedicated five hours and more a day to public affairs. His instinct for orderliness, his love of small detail, and the punctual routine with which he applied himself to his tasks sat easily with him. "His ministers," said Michelet, "might change or die; he, always the same, went through his duties, ceremonies, royal fêtes, and the like, with the regularity of the sun, which he had chosen as his emblem." While he might have been more willing that many other monarchs to devote so much time to matters of government, his enthusiasm was not matched by any real sense of compassion for those he governed. "His whole reign passed without his ever showing any real feeling for his poor subjects; and his indifference to the health and feelings of those nearest him, his treatment of the court, especially of the ladies of it, was such as nothing but their abject fear of him, and the meanness engendered by the atmosphere of such a court, could explain." [31]

To Louis, people were there to be ruled: an attitude typified by the increase in the African slave trade during his rule – with the number of galleys in the French navy rising from six to forty, each able to hold two hundred slaves. To man these galleys the French used Turks captured in the Barbary wars or young French criminals accused of capital offences, condemned to the galleys for life instead of execution. Furthermore, the colonial ambitions pursued by Louis's finance minister Jean-Batiste Colbert in New France (the French possessions in North America) and the enslavement of the Iroquois[38] by Donnenville to serve in the galleys reinforced a resentment towards the French which was to bear fruit in the seventeenth and eighteenth centuries. The contest for control of the North American continent between France and Great Britain would ultimately be decided by the choice the Iroquois made between them. [39]

Louis's desire for absolute power over his subjects did not allow for interference by the Pope, and he set out to curb the latter's influence in the internal affairs of France. He convoked a great assembly of the clergy which sought to establish the 'liberties' of the French church, but these were in effect liberties of the church in its relationship to the Pope, not in relationship to the royal power. The articles agreed upon included a recognition of the independent authority of the secular power, and a denial of Papal infallibility. The conflict between Louis and Pope Innocent XI would play its own part in the unusual alliance eventually organised against France.

Louis XIV

Not unlike many powerful men before him, and many since, Louis was obsessed with images of his own grandeur. "In my heart, I desire, more than anything else, more than life itself, an illustrious reputation... The one emotion which overpowers all others in the minds of kings is the sense of their own greatness and glory." Apart from the splendour of his court at Versailles, Louis felt such 'greatness and glory' could also be achieved through the territorial enlargement of France. Indeed, his reign had got off to a propitious start, when in 1643 French arms utterly defeated the world-famous Spanish infantry. "The battle of Recroi destroyed for ever the older fighting power of the world, the Spanish foot, and gave to France her first taste of that military glory which marks the reign; it was the *baptême de feu* of the child-king of France." [31]

When the new office of commissary-general of fortifications was instituted in 1677, and Vauban was appointed, a new phase was marked in Louis's pursuit of territorial expansion. Vauban began to construct a string of fortifications around France's frontiers, strongholds which would serve not just in the defence of France but as springboards for attack. Finding that such a line of defences required some territory not under his control, Louis initiated a policy known as 'reunions' by which he used old feudal concepts regarding 'dependencies' to bring such territories under his control. He conquered Franche Comté, widened his hold on Alsace, and in

1681 prised Strasbourg away from Germany, desirous of that ancient Teutonic city to consolidate his eastern frontier. French soldiers moved into the new territories, more fortifications were constructed, and before the concerned eyes of Europe the frontiers of France were slowly pushed into Germany. By secret agreement Louis also became master of Casale, which gave him an influence in Italy. To the north the French army captured Luxembourg and extensive areas of the Spanish Netherlands.

Further opportunity presented itself when the Elector of the Palatinate, an area in western Germany touching both the Rhine and the Danube, died childless. Louis immediately claimed the territory for France. This time, however, he had gone too far. Such a move would have brought Louis right into the heart of Germany. Those who had watched his territorial acquisitions with increasing alarm hesitated no longer. In July 1686 was signed the League of Augsburg. The Emperor (of what still survived of the Holy Roman Empire), the King of Spain, the Dutch, the elector of Saxony, the Palatinate elector, and a number of lesser princes, all joined it. The heart and soul of the League was William of Orange. The following year, after Louis occupied the papal territory of Avignon during a period of conflict between himself and the pope, the latter secretly acceded to the League. Whatever might have united the two men in religion, Pope Innocent XI believed Louis and his schemes posed a real threat to Europe. "It is a strange moment in history in which the pope and the emperor, the king of Spain and the elector of Bavaria, unite to resist the advance of Catholic France and the Catholic king of England." [31]

For two years the League remained solely on the defensive, but it was clear that hostilities could not long be avoided. It was Louis who decided to act, but instead of marching against Holland, which would have created a direct threat to William of Orange and prevented William from acting against James II of England, he decided to make his move along the Rhine. A French garrison was sent to occupy Cologne, the army took Philipsburg and the Palatinate and the three Rhine electorates fell easily under Louis's control.

William, his hands free now that French energies were directed elsewhere, set sail for England and James II was bloodlessly deposed, fleeing to the protection of Louis in France. Louis realised his error and withdrew from the Palatinate, though not before his soldiers subjected it to a "scathing of fire and sword" which enraged the feelings of the Germans and instilled a new purposefulness into the alliance against Louis.

Louis furnished James with a strong force of soldiers and ships, and when the latter landed in Ireland almost the whole island declared for him. However, William arrived in hot pursuit and at the Battle of the Boyne checked this threat to his flank.

> It was not too soon. A very few days after the battle of the Boyne, Tourville, commanding the French fleet, had defeated the Anglo-Dutch navy off Beachy Head; and in the same month, Marshal Luxembourg won the battle of Fleurus from Waldeck with his German and Dutch troops. In Piedmont Catinat inflicted a grave defeat on Victor Amadeus at Staffarda. Still, the war of 1690 was in the end indecisive, thanks to the battle of the Boyne. [31]

However, this is anticipating events somewhat; let us now turn to political developments in England.

7

— The 'Glorious Revolution' —

On 6 February 1685, Charles II of England died. Although at heart he had long been a Roman Catholic – and was formerly reconciled with Catholicism on his deathbed – in the latter part of his reign he had sought to work in alliance with England's Protestant establishment, with government in his last years being based upon a close understanding between his royal Court and with the Tory Party and High Church. Charles was succeeded as King by his younger brother James, who had converted to Catholicism in 1672. This fact – when set alongside the anti-Catholic fears then prevalent in England, and the widespread belief that Catholicism was synonymous with all that was abhorrent in the France of Louis XIV – had led three separate Houses of Commons during Charles's reign to vote to exclude James from succession to the throne. However, Charles, through patient and shrewd efforts, had managed to preserve the hereditary nature of the monarchy, and his brother's accession to the throne, as James II, proceeded unopposed.

At first, James, who has been described as "fanatical, humorless and oversexed",[40] proceeded with circumspection and caution. Although he had initially promised that he would "endeavour to preserve this government both in church and state as it is by law established", in reality he was determined to do all he could to promote Catholicism throughout his realm.

However, before James could proceed with implementing any of his designs, a rebellion was raised by the Duke of Monmouth, natural son of Charles II, and a claimant to the throne. However, this ill-fated rebellion was crushed at the Battle of Sedgemoor on 15 July 1685. As Trevelyan wrote:

> The revenge taken upon the rebels, first by Kirke and his barbarized soldiers from Tangier, and then by Judge Jeffreys in his insane lust for cruelty, was stimulated by orders from the King. It was the first thing in the new reign that alarmed and

disgusted the Tories. In the general horror felt at the long rows of tarred and gibbeted Dissenters along the roadsides of Wessex, came the first recoil from the mutual rage of parties that had so long devastated English political and religious life, the first instinctive movement towards a new era of national unity and toleration. [32]

James II

The defeat of the rebellion and his peaceful accession to the throne emboldened James in his purpose, in which he was encouraged by his close ally, Louis XIV. The rebellion gave him the excuse to keep a standing army of 30,000, part of which was encamped at Hounslow Heath in an attempt to overawe the capital. Without consulting Parliament he suspended the laws against Catholics and Dissenters – this allowed him to appoint Roman Catholic officers in the army and navy, and to include them among his Privy Councillors.

In 1685 the Privy Council, the rural and municipal magistrates, the Lords Lieutenant and the Sheriffs, had been almost without exception Tories and High Churchmen. Within a few years these Tories and High Churchmen were to find themselves systemically ousted from their political powerbases as James attempted to replace them with Roman Catholics.

Protestants arriving from Ireland, where James's Romanising policies had been much more extensive and successful, further inflamed the fears of England's Protestant majority as to James's intentions. However, these fears were not primarily religious. Protestants feared the political implications of English Catholicism more than its theology; they feared the absolute nature of its claim to represent the ultimate in social order more than its specific ceremonies; but most of all they began to fear for their country's parliamentary system of government. Unheedful of his subjects' fears, James's Romanising policy continued apace.

The King now openly attacked the possessions and freeholds of the Anglican clergy. The Court of High Commission was revived

58

The seven bishops on their way to the Tower

contrary to law, as the King's instrument for dragooning the Church. The Fellows of Magdalen, Oxford, were illegally deprived of their property and their great College was turned into a Roman Catholic seminary. The effect of this tyranny was very great upon Oxford and on all who looked to Oxford for their opinions. It transformed the citadel of non-resistance and divine right into a rebel town, that flew the Orange colours in the High Street during the most eventful winter in English history. [32]

In April 1688 James raised the stakes still further. He ordered that his Declaration of Indulgence, by which he had suspended the laws against Roman Catholics and Dissenters, be read out in every church in England on successive Sundays in May and June. The leaders of the Church of England felt they could not acquiesce any longer. The Archbishop of Canterbury and six bishops refused and were immediately sent to the Tower of London prior to their trial for sedition. On 30 June, much to James's fury, the bishops were acquitted by the jury and the London mob celebrated by burning effigies of the pope. That night a letter signed by seven leading establishment figures was sent secretly to Holland, inviting William of Orange to come over and help preserve the religion, liberties and properties of Englishmen.

The decision to rebel against the King had gained added momentum when a son had been born to James on 10 June. This new Prince of Wales now stood next in line to the throne, ahead of James's two children by his first marriage, Mary and Anne, who had remained Protestant, Mary also being married to William of Orange. The fact that James's Catholic line would now continue after his death alarmed his opponents, and even fuelled doubts surrounding the new-born infant:

> The baby's birth was a month premature and immediately gave rise to rumours that he was not the king's son but a fraudulent changeling, smuggled into the lying-in chamber in a warming-pan, on instructions from the Jesuits. The fact that the child was a healthy boy took everybody by surprise; Mary Beatrice had had children but they had died in infancy and she had not given birth for six years. Events around the birth helped fan the flames of suspicion: almost all those present in the room were Catholics and those who should have been there as witnesses, notably the Archbishop of Canterbury, the Earls of Clarendon and Rochester (staunch Anglicans and uncles of Mary and Anne) and the Dutch ambassador, were excluded. [35]

On 1 November, 1688, William Henry, Prince of Orange and Nassau, Captain-General of the Republic of the United Netherlands, set sail with a Dutch armada of fifty warships and two hundred transports. This development was welcomed by Pope Innocent XI, a man of moderation who disapproved of the policy being pursued by James, and who helped finance William's army. "Innocent had quarrels of his own with Louis XIV and the French Jesuits; he dreaded the French power in Italy and in Europe, and therefore watched with sympathy the sailing and the success of William's Protestant crusade, because it would release England from the French vassalage. What the Pope and the moderate English Catholics

William of Orange

hoped to obtain in England was not political supremacy but religious toleration." [32]

The expedition was a risky venture. Tactics and heavy winds dictated that the Dutch fleet disembark along the unguarded south-west coast rather than the closer south-east coast. James's naval commander moved too late to make an interception and William's army disembarked unopposed on 5 November. William declared for a free Parliament... and then waited. As each day passed James's position grew ever more precarious, with desertions from his army, armed rebellion in the north of England, and the civil population and many leading establishment figures rallying to the Williamite cause. Racked by doubt and alarm James finally decided to abandon his kingdom and flee to France. When he arrived in St Germains, Louis XIV received him with much pomp and provided him with a substantial income. William's response to Louis's kindness towards his father-in-law was less than generous: "When he has dragged that corpse around for three or four years, he will be as much embarrassed by him as I have been." [35]

The bloodless revolution was complete, although, as Maurice Ashley reminds us:

> It is necessary to distinguish the motives of William from those of the conspirators who invited him over. William wanted to ensure that the English kingdom would not again closely ally itself with France, as it had done in 1670, to destroy the Dutch Republic and enhance the overweening power of Louis XIV. William was able to exercise his authority [as sovereign] by persuading the English parliament to unite with the Dutch States-General in a grand alliance to resist the aggressions of Louis XIV. As a contemporary statesman observed, 'he took England on the way to France'. [40]

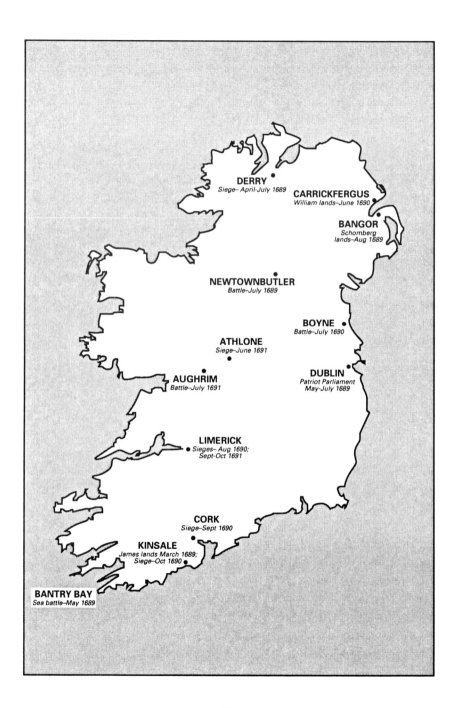

DERRY
Siege– April-July 1689

CARRICKFERGUS
William lands–June 1690

BANGOR
Schomberg lands–Aug 1689

NEWTOWNBUTLER
Battle–July 1689

BOYNE
Battle–July 1690

ATHLONE
Siege–June 1691

DUBLIN
Patriot Parliament May-July 1689

AUGHRIM
Battle–July 1691

LIMERICK
Sieges– Aug 1690; Sept-Oct 1691

CORK
Siege–Sept 1690

KINSALE
James lands March 1689; Siege–Oct 1690

BANTRY BAY
Sea battle–May 1689

8

— The War in Ireland —

When James II ascended the throne of England the inhabitants of the growing town of Belfast (population around 2,000) sent a congratulatory address to the new King. However, doubts soon surfaced when it became clear that James, as an avowed Roman Catholic, was determined to adopt rapid methods of Romanizing his realm. The fears of the Protestant population in Ireland were first engendered by the recall of Ormonde, the Lord Lieutenant, whose Protestant sympathies were not in accord with James's design for the island.

Although in England James had to tread warily, in Ireland he felt he could proceed as intended. In 1686 he appointed Richard Talbot, an ardent Roman Catholic, Earl of Tyrconnell and General of the Forces in the island. Tyrconnell proceeded to dismiss all 'Englishmen' from the army, disband the Protestant regiments and replace them with Roman Catholics. In January 1687 Tyrconnell became Lord Lieutenant of Ireland. It was well known that his ultimate intention was to drive all the recent settlers out of Ireland, to destroy the Protestant faith in general, and to restore the Irish aristocracy.

Although loyalty to James began to decline in England, the civil power of Catholics increased in Ireland. By the autumn of 1688 all the judges in Ireland were Catholics as were almost all the highest officers of the State. The brewing constitutional crisis in England engendered by James's policies was not paralleled in Ireland where Tyrconnell still held the country firmly for his king. Even in Ulster the Presbyterians "did not at once appear against the king's government". According to J. M. Barkley, "What settled the issue was Tyrconnell's 'sparing neither age nor sex, putting all to the sword without mercy' (to use the words of a survivor) following the Break of Dromore."[41]

James II lands in Ireland

Tyrconnell's policies were sooner or later bound to provoke resistance. When the regiment of Lord Mountjoy, one of the few essentially Protestant ones remaining, was ordered to leave Londonderry and be replaced by the Catholic MacDonnells under Lord Antrim, the limits had finally been reached. The citizens, fearing a repetition of the massacres of 1641, wanted to refuse the troops entry. However, as Robert Kee points out:

> Other voices, shocked, declared that it would be unthinkable to try and keep royal troops out of a royal garrison. The Protestant Bishop of Londonderry and other Protestant establishment figures were among the latter, although the Presbyterians with their naturally independent attitude to authority were less troubled by such scruples. The official decision, however, had been taken to admit the troops in the normal way, when suddenly thirteen apprentice boys of the city took matters into their own hands, seized the keys of the gates of Londonderry and on 7th December 1688 slammed them firmly in the face of lord Antrim's Redshanks – King James's troops. [42]

Enniskillen followed suit, and throughout Ulster, defence

associations were set up and councils of war elected. By the end of December James had fled England for France and on 13 February 1689 William and Mary were proclaimed King and Queen of England. Confident of the strength of the Jacobite cause in Ireland, Tyrconnell urged James to try and regain the throne from there, a course of action also encouraged by Louis XIV. At first reluctant, James II finally landed at Kinsale and on 18 April commenced the Siege of Londonderry, which lasted a total of 105 days, the longest in British history. During that time one third of the city's 30,000 inhabitants died of injuries, famine and disease. At last, on 28 July, Derry was relieved by the British ship *Mountjoy* and two other vessels.

Two aspects of the siege were to lodge deep within the Irish Protestant subconscious: firstly, a 'No Surrender!' determination to stand firm against any perceived threats to their heritage; secondly, "an awareness that however much the northern Protestant may need British help he is also on his own",[42] a feeling no doubt reinforced by the fact that the British ships which finally lifted the siege had been nearby right from the beginning, but hadn't been able to summon up the courage to act.

The Siege of Derry

Finally, on 14 June, 1690, King William landed at Carrickfergus to a rapturous welcome from the populace and bonfires were lit on the hills of Antrim and Down. William and his army commander Schomberg – who had been in Ireland since August 1689 – travelled together by coach into Belfast. The cosmopolitan entourage which accompanied William should have indicated quite clearly to the citizens of the town that the events which were now unfolding had a broader European dimension quite separate from any parochial interests of the Irish. As Jonathan Bardon remarked:

> Never before had Belfast greeted so many men of distinction – Godard van Reede, Baron de Ginkel of Utrecht; Hans Willem Bentinck, the king's close adviser; the Duke of Würtemberg-Neustadt, the German commander of the Danish force; Count Henry Nassau; Prince Georg of Daamstadt, brother of Christian V of Denmark; the Duke of Ormond; and many others.[43]

William had been forced to come to Ireland partly because of Schomberg's reluctance to confront the Jacobite army. Schomberg, now in his mid-seventies, seemed to have lost that energy which had sustained him throughout his long military career – he had served with the Dutch, Swedish, French and English armies. While encamped near Dundalk, taunting Jacobites had taken this inactivity as weakness, a 'weakness' further compounded by the death through fever and disease of over 7,000 of his troops.

William, however, had arrived to do battle, being heard to remark that he had not come to let the grass grow under his feet.[43] At Loughbrickland in County Down he reviewed an army composed of Protestants from all over Europe – Dutch, Danes, French, Germans, English, Scots, Irish, Swiss, Italians, Norwegians and Poles. His army also included an elite unit, the Dutch Blue Guards, who were Catholics. The European dimension was to be completed by James's Jacobite force of Irish, French, English, Germans and Dutch.

The Williamite army, amounting to some 36,000 men, marched south to find that James, with about 25,000 men, had taken up position on the south bank of the River Boyne to the west of Dundalk. William deployed his own army on the northern bank. It was while he was riding around in open view of the enemy and wearing full regalia – a habit which dismayed his commanders – that his whole enterprise almost ended there and then when a enemy shot tore through his coat wounding him in the shoulder blade. However, as soon as a dressing was applied to the injury William rode round his dismayed troops to be greeted by their loud acclamations.

Both sides kept up a cannonade the rest of the day, and that evening William made a final inspection by torchlight, giving his orders for the impending battle. William's resolution to attack across the river the following morning was not approved by all his commanders, least of all Schomberg, who retired to his tent muttering that he had been more used to give such orders than to receive them.[44]

The next morning, 1 July, was bright and cloudless, and the Williamites – each with a sprig of green in their hats for identification – commenced the Battle of the Boyne.

William's strategy was two-pronged: there was to be a direct frontal assault across the Boyne, while his right wing, under the command of one of Schomberg's son, was to march some miles up the river to Slane, in the hope of turning the enemy's left flank. The feint succeeded, and many of James's best troops were drawn away in an attempt to prevent the Williamites outflanking them, or, even worse, cutting off any possible line of retreat.

The centre of William's army, consisting almost exclusively of foot soldiers, now commenced their frontal assault and marched, ten abreast, into the river. As they neared the southern bank the difficulties of their task must have seemed only too apparent: a fortification had been made by French engineers out of the hedges and buildings and a breastwork had been erected close to the water's edge. But still William's troops, led by the Dutch Blue Guards, pressed forward and eventually began to prevail, with the Irish foot, to Tyrconnell's great dismay, falling back in confusion. The Irish and French cavalry hurried to retrieve the situation and engaged the Blue Guards in a desperate fight in the bed of the river. Further downstream they also began to drive the Danish brigade back and assaulted the Huguenot regiments so ferociously they too began to give ground. The cavalry's efforts were so vigorous and tenacious that Schomberg, watching from the bank, became alarmed, and without any defensive armour rode into the midst of the fray. Close by him the French Huguenots were falling back before James's French cavalry, and the gallant veteran endeavoured to rally them, by calling out in French: "Come on, gentlemen: there are your persecutors!" He was immediately surrounded by a number of the Irish cavalry and perished. Almost at the same time the Reverend George Walker, who had been Governor of Derry during the siege, was shot dead.

Schomberg meets his death at the Boyne

Just then William himself arrived with his cavalry. He rode to the head of a contingent from Enniskillen, one of whom nearly shot him by mistake in the heat of the battle. "Gentlemen," he said, "I have heard much of you. Let me see something of you."

> One of the most remarkable peculiarities of this man, ordinarily so saturnine and reserved, was that danger acted on him like wine, opened his heart, loosened his tongue, and took away all appearance of constraint from his manner. On this memorable day he was seen wherever the peril was greatest. One ball struck the cap of his pistol; another carried off the heel of his jackboot; but his lieutenants in vain implored him to retire to some station from which he could give his orders without exposing a life so valuable to Europe. His troops, animated by his example, gained ground fast.[44]

Inexorably the tide of battle turned in William's favour and the Jacobites began to retreat, though their cavalry still retired fighting obstinately. For the Jacobites the battle was lost, whole troops had been cut to pieces, one fine regiment had but thirty unwounded men left, and their king had abandoned them and was already fleeing back to the safety of France.

When news of William's victory reached Pope Alexander VIII, who was delighted at what was in effect a French defeat, he ordered torchlight processions in Rome in celebration, and *Te Deums* were sung in the Catholic cathedrals of Austria and Spain.

Following the Battle of the Boyne the military position in Ireland remained fluid. The Boyne has been described as one of the decisive battles of the western world, for it signalled to Europe defeat for the French and the Jacobites – but it was not the final victory of the war in Ireland. Neither was it a battle altogether characterised by the direction of the professional soldier but a magnificent drama portraying the personalities of the two kings each of whom caused problems for his own most able generals.

For if Sarsfield was betrayed by the cowardice of James, so Schomberg was dismayed by the almost foolhardy courage of William. The Prince of Orange's legendary bravery was matched by great military genius and soundness of judgement. At the Boyne his tactics were proved to have been correct. Yet, if the battle was won by William, the pursuit was not. The losses on both sides had been less than on any field of battle of equal importance and celebrity – fifteen hundred Jacobites and five hundred Williamites. William's physical infirmities, his wound in the early part of the battle and the fatigue he had endured exhorting his men, had made him incapable of further progress. The King could not do everything, but what was not done by him was not done at all. And so the French and Jacobites escaped to fight another day.

From October 1690 until May 1691 no military operation on a large scale was attempted in the Kingdom of Ireland. During that winter and the following spring the island was divided almost equally between the contending parties. The whole of Ulster, the greater part of Leinster, and about one third of Munster was now controlled by the Williamites; the whole of Connaught, the greater part of Munster and two or three counties of Leinster was still held by the Jacobites.

Continuous guerrilla activity persisted, however, along the rough line of demarcation. In the spring of 1691, James's Lord Lieutenant, Tyrconnell, returned to Ireland, followed by the distinguished French general Saint Ruth, who was commissioned as Commander-in-Chief of the Jacobite army. Saint Ruth was a man of great courage and resolution but his name was synonymous with the merciless suppression and torture of the Protestants of France.

The Marquess of Ruvigny, hereditary leader of the French Protestants, and elder brother of that brave Caillemot who had fallen at the Boyne, now joined the Dutch general Ginkel, who was strengthening the Williamite army at Mullingar. Ginkel first took Ballymore where he was joined by the Danish auxiliaries under the command of the Duke of Wurtemburg, and then the strategic town of Athlone.

Thus the stage was set for one of the fiercest battles of that age or any other. Determined to stake everything in a final showdown Saint Ruth pitched his camp about thirty miles from Athlone on the road to Galway. He waited for Ginkel on the slope of a hill almost surrounded by red bog, chosen with great judgement near the ruined castle of Aughrim.

Soon after 6 o'clock on the morning of 12 July, 1691, the Williamite army moved slowly towards the Jacobite positions. Delay was caused, however, by a thick fog which hung until noon and only later in the afternoon did the two armies confront each other. The Jacobite army of twenty-five thousand men had further protected themselves by the construction of a defensive breastwork. The Williamites, numbering under twenty thousand, advanced over treacherous and uneven ground, sinking deep in mud at every step. For two hours the Jacobites defended the breastwork with such resolution that, as evening was fast closing in, Ginkel began to consider a retreat. Saint Ruth was jubilant and pressed his advantage. However, Ruvigny and Mackay, with the Huguenot and British Cavalry, succeeded in bypassing the bog at a place where only two horsemen could ride abreast. There they laid hurdles on the soft ground to create a broader and safer path and, as reinforcements rapidly joined them, the flank of the Jacobite army was soon turned. Saint Ruth was rushing to the rescue when a cannonball took off his head. He was carried in secret from the field and, without direction, the Jacobites faltered. The Williamite infantry returned to their frontal attack with rugged determination and soon the breastwork was carried. The Jacobites retreated fighting bravely from enclosure to enclosure until finally they broke and fled.

This time there was no William to restrain the soldiers. Only four hundred prisoners were taken and not less than seven thousand Jacobites were killed, a greater number of men in proportion to those engaged than in any other battle of that time. Of the victors six hundred were killed, and about a thousand were wounded. If the night had not been moonless and visibility reduced by a misty rain, which allowed Sarsfield to cover the retreat, scarcely a Jacobite would have escaped alive.

Waiting in the wings with his own army was a remarkable character named Balldearg O'Donnell. He had arrived from Spain shortly after the Battle of the Boyne claiming to be a lineal descendant of the ancient Gaelic kings of Tyrconnell in Ulster. He also claimed to be the O'Donnell 'with a red mark' (*ball dearg*) who, according to ancient prophecy, was destined to lead his followers to victory. Many ordinary Ulster Catholics had flocked to his standard, causing great hostility on the part of Tyrconnell who saw him as a threat to his own earldom.

Balldearg thus remained aloof from the battle. He proceeded to join the standard of William with 1200 men on 9 September, 1691, and marched to assist in the reduction of the Jacobite town of Sligo. This garrison surrendered on 16 September, 1691, on condition that they were conveyed to Limerick. Balldearg remained loyal to William and later entered his service in Flanders, with those of his men who elected to follow him.

James vindictively blamed his courageous soldiers for his defeat: "When it came to a trial they basely fled the field and left the spoil to their enemies, nor could they be prevailed upon to rally, though the loss in the whole defeat was but inconsiderable: so that henceforth I never more determined to head an Irish army and do now resolve to shift for myself." [35] Yet, the reality was quite the opposite: "...it was their king that condemned the Irish to hopeless failure. He called them cowards, whereas the cowardice was really his own, and he deserted them in their utmost need. They repaid him with the opprobrious nickname of 'Sheemas-a-Cacagh', or Dirty James." [45] Many of the defeated Jacobite soldiers chose exile, and between 1691 and 1791 almost half a million such 'Wild Geese' left Ireland to form the famous Irish Brigades of armies throughout Europe, and of this number 50,000 fell in battle. James's general, Patrick Sarsfield, Earl of Lucan, became a Marshal of France; Marshal Charles O'Brien, Viscount Clare and Earl of Thomond, fought for the French at Fontenoy; Marshal Count James Roland Nugent commanded in the Austrian army, and his son Laval became a Marshal in the service of

King Ferdinand V of Spain; Marshal Maxmilian von Browne rose in the service of Maria Theresa of Austria and Marshal Peter de Lacy became famous throughout Europe and parts of Asia as a commander in the Russian Army of Tsar Peter the Great.

9

— Ireland Pays the Penalty —

Just as Ireland was merely one chess piece, albeit an important one, in the contest between William's League and Louis XIV of France, so also was James II's attempt to wrest control of the island merely a stepping stone in his efforts to regain the throne of England. He had little regard for the rights of the Irish as such, except in so far as they were of benefit to him and did not undermine English control over Ireland. Even while in exile after his defeat his plans for the future demonstrated his prejudices.

> James's feelings for the native Irish were explicit in instructions he wrote for his son in 1692: principle garrisons should never be entrusted to Irish governors or Irish troops; the sons of ancient families should be given an English education, to wean them from their hatred of the English; schools should be established to teach English and 'by degrees wear out the Irish language, which would be for the advantage of the body of the inhabitants'; the Os and Macs should be told that the estates declared forfeit by James I and his predecessors could not be restored; no native of Ireland should be lord lieutenant.[35]

When James had arrived in Ireland the conflict of interests between himself and the Irish leaders had soon become apparent: *they* were concerned above all with reversing the Cromwellian land settlement and James had been forced to summon an Irish parliament, which later became known as the 'patriot' parliament. In May 1689 this parliament, composed mainly of the 'Old English', or Anglo-Irish Catholics, had repealed the Act of Settlement and passed an act of Attainder against some 2,400 Protestant landowners. This had not been to James's liking – conscious of how English Protestant opinion would view such an action, he would have preferred to treat his Irish Protestant subjects more pragmatically. But James had been in no position to dictate a different course of events – he was reminded "If your Majesty will not fight for our rights, we will not fight for yours" – although he had insisted on the maintenance of 'Poynings' law'

73

which ensured Ireland's subordination to the English crown.

Shortly after his defeat at the Boyne, James fled back to the safety of France, assuming that the war in Ireland was lost. But the Irish Jacobites were made of stronger mettle than their worthless king and under the inspired leadership of Patrick Sarsfield a determined resistance was continued.

Although William of Orange possessed a strong religious conviction and a warm attachment to the Protestant faith, his Protestantism was not imbued with the intolerance exhibited by so many others of his time. This tolerance, aided no doubt by William's desire to bring the war in Ireland to a speedy resolution so that he could concentrate on affairs in mainland Europe, was evident in the negotiations conducted on his behalf with his Irish Catholic adversaries. His Dutch general, Ginkel, offered the Irish toleration for their religion and security for their property in return for surrender. Galway soon accepted the terms. In Limerick, after a week of negotiations, a generous bargain was struck. By the Treaty of Limerick the Irish officers and ordinary soldiers were permitted to choose between taking an oath of allegiance to William and returning to their estates or homes, enlisting in the English army, or departing into exile in France. The Catholic population in general were to enjoy the privileges "as they had enjoyed under Charles II and as were consistent with the laws of Ireland". Further, "all the inhabitants of Limerick or any other garrison now in the possession of the Irish... all the officers and men now in arms under commission of King James in the English quarters or the counties of Limerick, Clare, Kerry, Cork, Mayo (and Galway by separate capitulation) [and] all such as are under their protection in these counties", could retain their former estates, properties, privileges and professions on the condition they took the simple oath of Allegiance enacted in the English Parliament in the first year of William and Mary, *and no other*, that is, it did not include the oath of Supremacy or any abjuration of the papal spiritual power.

Such terms, especially for a defeated foe, were surprisingly generous. The problem was that the English establishment considered them far too generous. As Edmund Curtis pointed out: "While Ginkle could speak for William, both were foreigners who could not understand the place of the King in the new constitution of England, and it was soon shown that the English parliament meant to interpret the Treaty both in letter and spirit in the most narrow and ungenerous way."[46] This conflict of views on the elements in the Treaty was highlighted when a copy of the treaty reached William. The clause, "all such as are under their protection", which had wide-ranging implications, was found to have been somehow 'omitted', but William re-inserted it in his own handwriting. He himself considered the omission an accident, but it is unlikely that this was so.

William and the English establishment were to be at odds on other occasions, most notably after the war against Louis was successfully concluded, and the latter had agreed, in the Treaty of Ryswick in 1698, to recognise William as the lawful sovereign of England.

> As the war had cost £17,000,000, parliament resolved that all the troops raised since 1680 should be disbanded, and that the army should consist of only ten thousand men, while the ensuing year they not only voted that this number should be further reduced, but that no one but natural-born Englishmen should be allowed to serve. This resolution so irritated William, who was warmly attached to his Dutch guards and to the French protestants who had assisted him, that he entertained serious intentions of abdicating the throne and retiring to Holland.[47]

With the defeat of the Irish Catholic Jacobite cause, a new Lord Lieutenant for Ireland was installed in 1692 to represent the English Crown. He summoned an Irish parliament, this time a wholly Protestant body, and under its direction the attainders by which the 'Patriot' parliament had voted to dispossess thousands of Protestant landowners were now enacted in reverse. Under a Court of claims, some 4,000 Catholic landowners were attainted and their lands forfeited to the Crown. To the anger of both the English and Irish parliaments, William used his royal influence in favour of the attainted and managed to have land rights restored to sixty-five great landowners who were not protected by the Treaty of Limerick.[46]

'Catholic' ownership of the land was now to decline even further, not just because of the confiscations, but because many Catholic landowners thought it more prudent to relinquish their religion than their lands.

> It is reckoned that by 1700 the Roman Catholics had the freehold of about one-eighth of the land, but even this was to be greatly reduced in the next thirty or forty years by the proprietors conforming to the Established Church either willingly or under pressure of the Penal laws. Many great names had vanished by

the attainders of over fifty years; others now ceased to be leaders of the majority. The second Duke of Ormond was a Williamite; so was the Earl of Kildare; the Earl of Antrim in the next generation was a Protestant, and so it befell with other names such as MacMurrough Kavanagh. The 'Lords of the Pale' now only survived in a few timid Catholic peers such as the Earl of Fingall, while in Munster of the old nobility Browne, Earl of Kenmare, became the leading name. Of all the great Gaelic patronymics of 1500, only O'Brien, Earl of Inchiquin, finally remained in the peerage, but only as a supporter of Church and State.[46]

In 1695 the Irish parliament began to formulate the notorious Penal Code, which, in the way it treated the defeated Irish, violated both the spirit and the letter of William's Treaty of Limerick. William's sovereignty, however, thanks to the 'Glorious Revolution', now had to be shared with the English Parliament and his attempts to mitigate the penal laws were thwarted.

The penal laws were motivated more by political than by religious considerations. The war against Louis of France was still undecided and the large number of exiled Irish soldiers and Catholic Irish nobility in service with Louis posed the very real threat that the Jacobite cause in Ireland could be rekindled.

The supposed aim of the penal laws – to eradicate Catholicism in Ireland – was never seriously implemented, and little attempt was made to convert the mass of the people. The penal laws which *were* implemented, and with rigour, were those which aimed at keeping Catholics from attaining any positions of power – whether in parliament, government office, the legal profession, or the army or navy. This was achieved by making membership of these professions conditional on a qualifying oath, worded in such a manner that no sincere Catholic could possibly take.

Yet, just as with the great landowners, pragmatism often overrode devotion. "Great numbers of barristers and lawyers went over to the established church early in the [eighteenth] century, including John Fitzgibbon, father of the future earl of Clare, chief architect of the act of union."[48]

To the mass of the Irish people, however, whose poverty and hardship were not the result of penal laws but the product of social inequality and economic circumstance, it was probably of little practical relevance whether their subsistence living was ordained by Catholic *or* Protestant landlords. As so often before, they had been used as cannon-fodder in a war which had tried to win political power, the return of land, and the retention of wealth – not for them, but for others.

The economic precariousness of peasant existence, when later coupled with the devastating effects of the Great Famine, was to force one million Irish men and women to emigrate to America in search of a better future. But this was to occur over a century and a half later; it is ironic that, in the aftermath of the Williamite victory, it was a section of the 'victors' who were forced to see emigration to the New World as a panacea for their troubles.

10

— Reward for Loyalty —

The Protestants of Ulster had defended Derry and Enniskillen. They had saved Ireland for the British Crown. Yet all this passed for nothing. The English Church was Episcopalian and the 'Protestant Ascendancy' which established itself in Ireland following the 'Glorious Revolution' was thus actually an Episcopalian Anglo-Irish one, that is, the 'English in Ireland'. Having reduced the rebellious Catholics by the harsh Penal Laws, which were based on French Catholic legislation against Protestants, the High Church Party had gained in strength, and by the reign of Queen Anne (1702-1714) were pressing for complete conformity.

In 1704 the Test Act was passed which required all office holders in Ireland to take the sacrament of the Anglican Church. Although ostensibly passed to further discourage Catholicism, the real object of the Act was to place the Presbyterians on the same plane of impotence. Presbyterian ministers had now no official standing and marriages performed by them were null and void. To the High Churchmen they were actually inferior to Catholic priests, who were considered lawfully ordained in the line of apostolic succession. Presbyterians and other Dissenters could not now serve in the army, the militia, the civil service, the municipal corporations, the teaching profession or the commission of the peace. At Belfast the entire Corporation was expelled, and Londonderry lost ten of its twelve aldermen (Schism Act).

Yet for all that, the Presbyterians had long made their adjustment to religious restrictions, and most bishops of the Church of Ireland were especially tolerant in an age of bigotry. Indeed, Archbishop William King was prominent in his expression of abhorrence to the Archbishop of Canterbury, not only of the risks of increasing the alienation of the Presbyterians, but of English commercial avarice in restricting the Irish Woollen trade and the practice of rack-renting by landlords, whereby a farmer's land would be sold to the highest bidder when his lease ran out. The final straw came with the drought of the 'teen years of the 18th century. This ruined crops, including flax, so that farmers, weavers and townspeople suffered alike. In 1716 sheep were afflicted with the 'rot' and many died. Severe frosts ensued, prices soared and absentee English landlords steadily increased their rents. Thus began around 1717 the great migration from Ulster to America of those who were to become known in their new homeland as the 'Scotch-Irish'.

An earlier emigrant to America had been Francis Mackemie, born of Scottish parents near Ramelton, County Donegal. He settled in Eastern Virginia, and in 1706 was one of the most prominent members of the first Presbytery founded in America. Mackemie is justly considered to be the founding father of the Presbyterian Church in America, which was well organised to receive the new Ulster immigrants.

Soon Ulster people were settling in New York State, where they founded the Orange and Ulster counties. The first wave of migration to Pennsylvania (1717-1718) was enough to arouse the English conscience and in 1719 an Act of Parliament was passed to permit Dissenters to celebrate their own form of worship. But rack-renting continued and from 1725 to 1729 there was such an exodus of Ulster Presbyterians to the south-eastern tier of counties in Pennsylvania that their political influence was quickly becoming considerable. That influence was directed increasingly against England. A 'feed-back' into Ulster itself helped to make it a centre of radicalism, which was embodied in the establishment of one of the world's first daily newspapers, the *Belfast News Letter* in 1737. By 1738 Scotch-Irish settlers had pioneered their way from Pennsylvania into Virginia, of which two modern counties, Augusta and Rockbridge, claim to be the most Scotch-Irish in the present United States. By 1738 their Orange County, with its country seat in the Piedmont, embraced most of the Valley of Virginia, and also much of what is now West Virginia.

The winter of 1739-40 was known in Ulster as 'the time of the black frost', because of the darkness of the ice and the lack of sunshine. This severe weather caused famine all over the island, and a further wave of migration from Ulster (1740-1741). The new arrivals in America now generally went through Pennsylvania down into the Valley of Virginia. Here the McDowell family especially distinguished themselves, and thus did the Ulstermen become the men of Shenandoah. Others crossed the first range of the Alleghenies to settle in the valleys of (present) Highland and Bath counties.

In *America's Historylands*, a celebration of the rich historical heritage of America, due acknowledgment is given to the pioneering efforts of these Ulster settlers:

> Immigrants first settled the over-mountain country: Germans, English, Highlanders, Irish, Welsh, Scotch-Irish. New England stock seasoned the mixture. Dominant were the Scotch-Irish, defiant and aggressive, who seldom neglected an opportunity to better themselves. They had undying confidence in their manhood, were as bold as the Romans, and as Indian fighters won even the Shawnee's admiration. They were Presbyterians, though in the wilderness many turned Baptist or Methodist. They believed in freedom and equality, resented class distinction and the leisurely life. They "preferred the useful to the beautiful and even required the beautiful to be useful." They contributed mightily to the democratization of the United States.
>
> Of Scotch-Irish stock was James Robertson, who founded a settlement (the site of present Elizabethton, Tennessee) on the banks of the Watauga River. For mutual protection against Indians and outlaws, the Wataugans in 1772 formed the first independent government established by white men west of the Appalachians. During the Revolution they placed themselves under the mantle of North Carolina, but had to beat off attack after attack by England's Indian allies. In 1779 Robertson recruited a party and led them down the frozen Cumberland River. On snow-covered bluffs they founded Nashboro (Nashville). After the war the Wataugans' Scotch-Irish blood boiled because North Carolina continued to ignore their needs, indeed referred to the settlers as "off-scourings of the earth". In 1784 the Wataugans resolved to break away, "forming ourselves into a separate government." [49]

The resulting State of Franklin kept its independence for four years before finally succumbing because of economic hardship. However, this one example of a Scotch-Irish settlement highlights the tenaciousness of purpose and the independence of attitude which these settlers brought to their new country of domicile.

By the end of 1775 at least a quarter of a million Ulster men and women had left Ireland over a period of 58 years, and, according to some estimates, formed one sixth of the total population of the American Colonies. To America they brought a hatred of that aristocratic landlordism exemplified by the Marquis of Donegall, who had evicted many of the small farmers who couldn't pay the increased rents on his County Antrim estates. James Logan, the Provincial Secretary, had originally invited his fellow Ulstermen to Pennsylvania but soon complained that "a settlement of five families from the north of Ireland gives me more trouble than fifty of any other people." He found the Scotch-Irish "troublesome settlers to the government and hard neighbours to the Indians."

Indeed, the first armed clash to precede the Revolutionary War occurred in 1771 when Scotch-Irish settlers fought British forces on the Alamance River in North Carolina. On 20 May 1775 they were the most prominent signatories of the Mecklenburg Declaration of Independence drawn up in Charlotte, North Carolina. They subsequently supported the Declaration of Independence passed by the Continental Congress on 4 July 1776 and they composed the flower and backbone of Washington's army in the Revolutionary War which followed.

The Official Declaration of Independence was written in the handwriting of Charles Thompson from Maghera, printed by John Dunlap from Strabane, given its first public reading by the son of an Ulsterman, Colonel John Nixon, and among the signatories were the following, all either born in Ulster, or born to Ulster parents – John Hancock, President of the Congress, Thomas McKean, Thomas Nelson, Robert Paine, Edward Rutledge, George Taylor, Matthew Thornton and William Whipple. The great Seal of the United States – an eagle holding arrows and a branch – was designed by Charles Thompson after a Congressional committee consisting of Franklin, Jefferson and Adams, broke up in disagreement. Edward Rutledge's brother John chaired a committee of five states which drew up the United States Constitution. According to Alexis de Tocqueville, the United States Constitution bore Rutledge's "personal stamp. One man made it; and it was Rutledge."

The revolutionary cause was advocated by the *Belfast News Letter,* and the contemporary Harcourt wrote that "The Presbyterians in the north are in their hearts Americans." A German captain who fought alongside the British redcoats was quite explicit: "Call this war by whatever name you may, only call it not an American rebellion; it is nothing more or less than a Scotch-Irish Presbyterian rebellion." The Pennsylvania Line, the famous force of regular troops, was of primarily Ulster descent. George Washington said, "If defeated everywhere else I will make my last stand for liberty among the Scotch-Irish of my native Virginia." The birthplace of New York state was the Ulster County courthouse, burned in 1777 by the British, who were aided by the Iroquois Indians under their Mohawk hero-chieftain, Brant.

Another direct influence on the radical thinking which culminated so dramatically in the 'New World' was the work of the great Ulster philosopher, Francis Hutcheson, son of an Armagh Presbyterian minister, and who was born probably at Drumalig, Saintfield, County Down in 1694. He studied for the church at Glasgow (1710-1716) but then started a private academy in Dublin where he was particularly associated with the advanced Presbyterian libertarians, Thomas Drennan, William Bruce and Samuel Haliday. In 1729 he was appointed professor of Moral Philosophy at Glasgow, where he died in 1746. His most important work is *A Sense of Moral Philosophy*. Hutcheson was quite explicit about the right of resistance by the people in the event of a betrayal of trust by a government. He expounded the doctrine of religious toleration and he deeply admired the tradition of armed militias for the protection of civil liberties. The principles he espoused found their way via American revolutionary thinkers into the Declaration of Independence and are embodied in the American Constitution. Hutcheson's influence on Thomas Jefferson, John Adams and others is explored in M. White's *Philosophy of the American Revolution* and G. Wills' *Inventing America*. In fact, Wills concluded that Hutcheson's influence on Jefferson was stronger than that of John Locke.

James G. Leyburn's study of Scotch-Irish influence on the formation of the early United States includes the following assessment:

> Weber's idea of the Protestant ethic and Tawney's of the connection between Protestantism and the rise of capitalism do not find their most convincing example in the Scotch-Irish; nevertheless, like other Calvinists, they believed in self-reliance, improving their own condition in life, thrift and hard work, the taking of calculated risks. They believed that God would prosper His elect if they, in turn, deserved this material reward by their conscientious effort. Farmers though they generally were, neither they nor their ancestors had been peasants in the sense of blind traditionalism of outlook. Their optimistic self-reliance, with a conviction that God helps those who help themselves, was to become the congenial American folk philosophy of the next century, not far removed from materialism and a faith in progress.

The Scotch-Irish were no more the originators of these American convictions than they had been the originators of the idea of freedom and individualism. What is significant is that, holding the attitude they did, and being present in such large numbers throughout most of the United States, they afforded the middle ground that could become typical of the American as he was to become. The Scotch-Irish element could be the common denominator into which Americanism might be resolved. [50]

11

— In Retrospect —

For many generations to come the Revolution of 1688-9 was spoken of... as 'the glorious revolution'. Its glory did not consist in any deed of arms, in any signal acts of heroism on the part of Englishmen, nor in the fact that a whole nation proved itself stronger than one very foolish King. There was indeed a certain ignominy in the fact that a foreign fleet and army, however friendly and however welcome, had been required to enable Englishmen to recover the liberties they had muddled away in their frantic faction feuds. The true 'glory' of the British Revolution lay in the fact that it was bloodless, that there was no civil war, no massacre, no proscription, and above all that a settlement by consent was reached of the religious and political differences that had so long and so fiercely divided men and parties.[32]

During William's reign the National Debt was commenced, the Bank of England established, the modern system of finance introduced, ministerial responsibility recognised, the standing army transferred to the control of parliament, the liberty of the press secured and the British constitution established on a firm basis. [51] The removal of James from the throne of his kingdom had received the approval of many of the radical English philosophers of the day, some of whom had returned from exile as participants in, or in the wake of, the Revolution.

Among these radicals it was John Locke whose ideas provided the best theoretical justification for the 'Glorious Revolution'. Locke's *Two Treatises of Government* sought to establish the basis for legitimate government. He first set out to discredit the argument that a king's power was divine and not limited by human law, insisting that, on the contrary, the Bible prescribed no particular form of government, this could only be determined by the people themselves. Locke went further and claimed that "it is lawful for the people... to resist their king" when the monarch put his private interests above the· interests of the community as a whole. "I say using force upon the people, without authority and contrary to the trust put in him that does so, is a state of war with the people, who have a right to *reinstate* their legislative in the exercise of their power."

Not only was Locke's thinking important in its European context – the English Revolution had a profound impact on French liberalism – it was an important influence upon the radicals who made the American Revolution of 1776; indeed, his *Two Treaties of Government* has been called "the textbook of the American Revolution".

The voice of popular democracy had also been making itself heard with increasing articulateness. The radical Leveller movement felt that because the power of parliament was ultimately derived from the people it was the people therefore who were sovereign – parliament only possessed a purely delegated authority. Another group, the Diggers, believed that it was private property, particularly land ownership, which was at the root of all social evil and inequality, and their main spokesman, Gerrard Winstanley, depicted the rule of kings as being no different from that of thieves. In 1649, forty years before the poor of Ireland would spill their blood for the sake of two competing kings, their more radical counterparts in England were attempting to seize and cultivate common land, in order that they could distribute the produce among the ordinary people.

Such radical ideas, and the profound changes they inaugurated were not, of course, simply a reaction to uniquely English events, but reflected fundamental social, economic and political changes occurring within European society in general. Increasingly, political struggles within society became more closely identified with the particular social and economic interests of different groups, even to the extent of overriding traditional allegiances.

For example, in America the 'Scotch-Irish', largely Ulster Presbyterian in origin, threw themselves wholeheartedly into the Republican camp – an ironic situation when viewed from today's perspective – believing that an independent American Republic was eminently more desirable for their social and economic wellbeing than continued control and interference by Britain. However, the growing economic and political power of these new republicans proved threatening to other sections of American society, who stayed decidedly Loyalist, including many Catholic Jacobites from the Highlands of Scotland, who had fought the House of Hanover in the

1745 rebellion and remembered the defeat of 1715, but who became staunch Loyalists because of the generous treatment they received in America from their former adversaries. Various 'cultural minorities', fearful of an increase in the power of the majority, often sought British help or protection – New Rochelle, for example, the only place where the French Calvinists still spoke French, was an area of substantial Huguenot Loyalism.

Nor were America's Black population convinced that an alliance with radical republicans was really to their advantage. Most of the Black community were "strongly attached to the British", according to one contemporary Loyalist source. Certainly there was a widespread fear of Black people among the newly consolidating American 'establishment', partly an extension of the perennial dread of slave revolt, and intensified by the mass desertion of slaves in response to a wholesale British offer of freedom.

Indeed, a strong disapproval of Black slavery was the most glaring omission from the Declaration of Independence. Matthew T Mellon, in his study of the racial attitudes of America's 'Founding Fathers', *Early American Views on Negro Slavery*, concluded that while the leading men at the time of the Revolution were all concerned with how to abolish the slave trade, economic pressures and moral indifference prevented them from energetically pursuing its abolition.

As the American Revolution gained momentum, the Indian peoples made some attempt at neutrality, but generally they favoured the British Government. They had no enthusiasm for the westward-pushing, uncontrollable colonial settlers who coveted their lands, and believed that the British, rather than the Americans, would be the most likely to seek restraints over this movement. Nothing highlights this allegiance better than the careers of the prominent 'Loyalists' who emerged from among the Mohawk people, such as John Deserontyon, Aaron Hill and Joseph Brant, who commanded the Iroquois nations with great skill on the British side during the Revolutionary War. Even today Chief Earl Hill of the Tyendinaga Mohawk Nation still professes that his people "were proud of their status and designation as United Empire Loyalists".

A delegation from the Mohawk nation came to Ulster in 1990 to attend the tercentenary celebrations of the Battle of the Boyne. During their visit they were no doubt made aware of the divisions which still run deep within Irish society as a consequence of that battle. This division must have seemed quite unnecessary to them, for in their own communities – in which Orange Lodges sit alongside self-help workshops – Protestants and Catholics are fully integrated and work together as Mohawks. It is surely high time that the communities in Ulster began that same process of integration, so that a new generation might finally escape the burden which our past history has for too long imposed upon us. As Chief Dan George reminded us:

> What wonders are children expecting while we hand them our problems?
> What hopes do we nourish in them while we are leading them into despair? [52]

Before I end this reassessment of 1690 and the Boyne, one question remains unanswered – what of Louis XIV and his grand design for France's territorial enlargement? Despite initial French successes Louis's war had eventually exhausted his country's resources and he was forced to concede defeat. Through the Treaty of Ryswick in 1697 he relinquished all the German territories, though he retained Strasbourg; he was forced to accept Dutch garrisons in the frontier towns of the Spanish Netherlands; and he agreed to recognise William of Orange as the rightful King of England.

While the French monarchy was to survive this defeat for another century – and indeed, see its character and style imitated by other European monarchies – its absolutist nature could not indefinitely withstand the pressures growing within European society, and under attack from the popular demands of the impoverished populace on the one hand and the ambitions of the privileged classes on the other, it was finally engulfed in the great cataclysm of the Revolution of 1789.

One legacy of Louis's reign contains a vivid lesson for us today. During the Second World War five thousand Jews, many of them children, found sanctuary in the village of Le Chambon-sur-Lignon, not far from William's former principality of Orange in the south of France, at that time under the control of the collaborationist Vichy government. The villagers, mostly French Huguenots whose forebears had suffered religious persecution under Louis and who "remained conscious of their position as outsiders in French society",[53] defied their government and built up a network of people who sheltered Jews in their homes and farmhouses. In this task they were assisted by nearby Roman Catholic convents and monasteries.

The Huguenots of Le Chambon-sur-Lignon, in co-operation with their Catholic neighbours, had demonstrated by their selfless actions their belief that the wellbeing of each and every part of any community is the responsibility of everyone, and all forms of oppression and violence can be confronted by that community working together in a spirit of mutual support and respect.

Even our study of history can become an integral part of this sharing process, as Mikhail Bakunin pointed out:

> Let us then never look backward, let us look ever forward. If it is permissible, and even useful and necessary, to turn back to study our past, it is only in order to establish what we have been and must no longer be, what we have believed and thought and must no longer believe or think, what we have done and must do nevermore.... The great, the real goal of history, its only legitimate objective, is the humanisation and emancipation, the real liberty, the prosperity and happiness of each individual living in society.

Sources

1   Sally Belfrage, *The Crack–A Belfast Year,* Andre Deutsch, 1987.
2   Jim Cusack, 'Project seeks common heritage', *Irish Times,* 23.07.83.
3   Peter C Woodman, *The Mesolithic in Ireland,* British Archaeological Report 58, 1978.
4   Séan P O Ríordáin, *Antiquities of the Irish Countryside,* Methuen, 1973.
5   John Waddell, 'The Question of the Celticization of Ireland', *Emania,* No. 9, 1991.
6   Liam de Paor, 'The People of Ireland', *The People of Ireland,* edited by Patrick Loughrey, Appletree Press/BBC, Belfast, 1988.
7   J P Mallory, 'The Origins of the Irish', *The Journal of Irish Archaeology,* II, 1984.
8   Peter Woodman, 'Prehistoric Settlers', *The People of Ireland,* edited by Patrick Loughrey, Appletree Press/BBC, Belfast, 1988.
9   Proinsias Mac Cana, 'Mongán Mac Fiachna and Immram Brain', in *Eriu,* vol XXIII, Dublin, 1972.
10 A T Q Stewart, *The Narrow Ground–Patterns of Ulster History,* Pretani Press, 1986.
11 Rev George Hill, *An Historical Account of the Plantation in Ulster at the Commencement of the Seventeenth Century 1608-1620,* Belfast, 1877.
12 F J Bigger, 'From Uladh to Galloway and From Galloway to Uladh', *The Red Hand Magazine,* vol 1 no 3, November 1920.
13 Estyn Evans, *The Personality of Ireland,* Blackstaff Press, Belfast 1981.
14 J M Roberts, *The Hutchinson History of the World.*
15 Rudolf Rocker, *Nationalism and Culture,* Michael E Coughlin, Minnesota, 1985.
16 Lloyd and Jennifer Laing, *Celtic Britain and Ireland – The Myth of the Dark Ages,* Dublin, 1990.
17 *Everyday Life through the Ages,* Reader's Digest, London, 1992.
18 Lewis Warren, 'The Normans', *The People of Ireland,* edited by Patrick Loughrey, Appletree Press/BBC, Belfast, 1988.
19 *The Joy of Knowledge,* Guild Publishing, London, 1980.
20 *quoted in* Ian Adamson, *Bangor–Light of the World,* Pretani Press, 1979.
21 G H Sabine, *A History of Political Theory,* George G Harrap, 1968.
22 *The Times Atlas of World History,* Times Books Limited, London, 1979.

23 Martin Luther, *quoted in* 20.

24 Norman Cohn, *The Pursuit of the Millennium*, Paladin, London, 1970.

25 Q Wright, 1965, *quoted in* 26.

26 Erich Fromm, *The Anatomy of Human Destructiveness*, Penguin, London, 1973.

27 Rev J A Wylie, *The History of Protestantism*, reprinted by Mourne Missionary Trust, Kilkeel, 1983.

28 John Romer, *Testament*, Michael O'Mara/Channel 4, 1988.

29 Francis Edwards, 'The Massacre of St Bartholemew's Eve', *Reform and Revolt*, 'Milestones of History' series, Newsweek Books, New York, 1974.

30 John Ardagh with Colin Jones, *A Cultural Atlas of France*, Amsterdam, 1991.

31 'History of France', Rev Dean Kitchin, *Encyclopaedia Britannica*, vol IX, ninth edition, Edinburgh, 1879.

32 G M Trevelyan, *A Shortened History of England*, Penguin, 1974.

33 *The Last Two Million Years*, The Reader's Digest, 1974.

34 Charles Wilson, 'Revolt of the Netherlands, *The Pen and the Sword*, 'Milestones of History' series, Newsweek Books, New York, 1974.

35 *Kings in Conflict–Ireland in the 1690s*, Ulster Museum, 1990.

36 John Laurence Carr, 'Revocation of the Edict of Nantes, *The Pen and the Sword*, 'Milestones of History' series, Newsweek Books, New York, 1974.

37 Philippe Erlanger, ' "L'état c'est moi" ', *The Pen and the Sword*, 'Milestones of History' series, Newsweek Books, New York, 1974.

38 Louis Hall, *A Short History of the Montréal Mohawk*, quoted in *This Land is Our Land: The Mohawk Revolt at Aka*, Craig Maclaine and Michael Baxendale, Montréal, 1990.

39 *Handbook of North American Indians, Volume 15: Northeast*, Washington, D.C., Smithsonian Institution, 1978.

40 Maurice Ashley, 'The Glorious Revolution', *The Pen and the Sword*, 'Milestones of History' series, Newsweek Books, New York, 1974.

41 J M Barkley, *Francis Mackemie of Ramelton*, The Presbyterian Historical Society of Ireland, Belfast, 1981.

42 Robert Kee, *Ireland–A History*, Sphere Books, 1982.

43 Jonathan Bardon, *A History of Ulster*, The Blackstaff Press, Belfast, 1992.

44 Lord Macauley, *History of England from the ascension of James II*, Macmillan & Co., 1913.

45 W K Sullivan and Richard Bagnell, 'A History of Ireland,' *Encyclopaedia Britannica*, vol XIII, ninth edition, Edinburgh, 1880.

46 Edmund Curtis, *A History of Ireland*, University Paperbacks, Methuen, London, 1968.

47 *The Imperial Dictionary of Universal Biography*, Vol. III, William Mackenzie, London.

48 Maureen Wall, 'The Age of the Penal Laws', *The Course of Irish History*, RTE/The Mercier Press, Cork, 1984.

49 *America's Historylands*, National Geographic Society, Washington DC, 1962.

50 James G Leyburn, *The Scotch–Irish: A Social History*, Chapel Hill, The University of North Carolina Press, 1962.

51 J O Thorne and T C Collocott, *Chambers Biographical Dictionary*, Cambridge, 1984.

52 Chief Dan George, *My Spirit Soars*, Hancock House Publishers, Canada, 1993.

53 Michael Berenbaum, *The World Must Know*, United States Holocaust Memorial Museum; Little, Brown and Company, USA, 1993.

Index